Crafts for the Home

MORE THAN
100 BEAUTIFUL DESIGNS
FOR THE HOME

Crafts
for the
Home

MORE THAN
100 BEAUTIFUL DESIGNS
FOR THE HOME

a Salamander book

Published by Salamander Books Limited
LONDON • NEW YORK

Published by Salamander Books Ltd.,
129-137 York Way,
London N7 9LG,
United Kingdom.

Salamander Books Ltd., 1993

ISBN 86101 729 3

Distributed by Hodder and Stoughton Services,
PO Box 6, Mill Road, Dunton Green,
Sevenoaks, Kent TN13 2XX.

CONTENTS

CREDITS

Craft Designs by: Caroline Green, Juliet Bawden, Cheryl Owen, Suzie Major, Susy Smith, Sarah
Waterkeyn, Mary Lawrence, Jan Hall and Joanna Sheen

Editor-in-Chief: Jilly Glassborow

Photographers: Steve Tanner, Di Lewis, Terry Dilliway and Jan Stewart

Typeset by: The Old Mill, London

Colour Separation by: Fotographics Ltd, London — Hong Kong, Scantrans Pte Ltd., Singapore
and Bantam Litho Ltd., England

Printed in Italy

INTRODUCTION

This beautiful book features more than 100 creative ideas for transforming your home using a wide range of craft techniques. It opens with an introduction to the variety of products currently available at specialist craft shops and department stores, and looks at the techniques involved in specific crafts. Following this, the section on Interior Design shows the variety of effects made possible by decorative paint finishes and the art of stencilling — find out how to completely transform a room. In the second chapter you can learn how to decorate furniture, perhaps giving old items a new look.

The fascinating art of fabric painting enables you to do everything from up-dating kitchen accessories to decorating roller blinds with trompe l'oeiul images. A variety of craft techniques can be used to make or decorate a range of fabulous household accessories — from a pleated paper lampshade to painted candlesticks. All techniques are easy to master, even by a beginner, so everyone will be able to produce impressive results first time.

For those who love entertaining, there are a wealth of ideas for creating impressive and elegant table settings, including decorating tablecloths, folded napkins and original and amusing place settings. In the section on Flower Decorations you can find out how to make a selection of beautiful fresh and dried flower arrangements, as well as learning how to decorate items such as a photo frame and a straw hat with dried flowers.

Every homecrafter wants to make Christmas really special and the last section of this book will inspire you to make a range of festive designs. There are lots of ways to decorate Christmas trees and even instructions on how to make a Christmas stocking. Festive designs made from fabric are a wonderful way to make decorations that last from year to year — so why not make a fabric wreath or festive topiary tree. For Christmas and New Year parties and dinners, there are also projects for some stunning table centrepieces.

You will find something here to suit every taste and level of dexterity, from easy projects for the less confident to complex designs for the more experienced. Each design is accompanied by colourful step-by-step photographs and easy-to-follow instructions on how to produce a successful result. Many of the projects can be done in an evening or a weekend. Where necessary, we have also provided patterns for you to follow, printed on grids so that you can easily convert them to the required size.

DECORATIVE PAINTING

Enhancing plain or rather ordinary household items with the art of decorative painting is a truly satisfying and highly individual pastime. As the picture opposite demonstrates, the scope of what you can paint is virtually limitless. Ceramic plates, tiles, vases, picture frames, glassware, lampshades or plain boxes can all be transformed with a little thought and skill.

Many of the techniques have been applied to small household or personal items, but in the early pages of this book, you will find numerous ways of enhancing architectural features and decorating rooms with stencilling techniques. Walls, arches, beams and even soft furnishings can be decorated and co-ordinated to create your very own personal decor.

MATERIALS

In recent years, manufacturers have met the demand of the hobbyist by supplying a vast range of paints, pens, crayons and varnishes through craft shops or good department stores. Although various products are intended for use on specific surfaces, you will find that some paints work well on more than one surface. Always use good quality brushes and clean them immediately after use. Brushes used with a solvent-based paint should be cleaned in white spirit or turpentine substitute; those used with water-based paint can be washed in water and a little detergent.

Acrylic Paints: Probably the most versatile, these water-based paints come in a wide range of bright colours, dry very fast to give a rich glossy finish, and unlike gloss paints, you don't have to prepare the surface first with primer or undercoat. They are fully waterproof and are suitable for both indoors and out.

Ceramic Paints: These are solvent-based paints designed for use on clay and pottery, though they are also suitable for glass, metal and wood. They come in a wide range of colours and give a glossy, opaque finish. Ideally, they should be used on items which receive little wear. Ceramic paints require at least 24 hours to dry, after which you can apply a coat of ceramic varnish to help protect the design.

Glass Paints: Also principally solvent-based that, when used on glass give a stained-glass effect. They can also be used on china and pottery to give a translucent finish. Glass paints are rather thick, sticky and difficult to apply, so they need some practice to apply correctly. They take at least 24 hours to dry (in a relatively dust-free environment). The item to be decorated must also be totally free from grease or dust before you begin which may mean washing well in warm soapy water then wiping with a cloth soaked in methylated spirits or petroleum

Plain items such as these are ideal for decorating, and there are paints available to suit any surface, be it wood, glass, ceramic, fabric or plastic.

essence. A second coat of paint may be necessary after the first has dried to achieve a strong enough colour. Water-based glass paints are also available.

Fabric Paints: There are various kinds available. Most need to be used on unbleached white or naturally coloured fabrics for the colours to remain true. However, there are paints available for use on dark fabrics; these tend to sit on top of the fabric as opposed to being absorbed by it.

Fabric paints must be 'fixed' so that the colours do not run when the fabric is washed. Manufacturers will recommend the method best suited for fixing their products; a common method is by heat.

Silk-paints: These can be used on wool as well as silk. In this book they have been used in conjunction with gutta, a gum-like substance which outlines each colour like lead outlines stained glass.

Varnishes: A coat of varnish will protect your paintwork. Polyurethane varnish is ideal for wood and comes in a matt or gloss finish. Ceramic varnish is specially designed for china or pottery. Other varnishes include crackle varnish which gives a crazed, 'antique' effect.

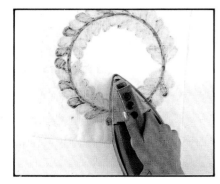

Far left: Most fabric paints can be fixed by ironing on the reverse of the design.

Centre: Some silk paints must be fixed in a special solution for five minutes, 48 hours after you have finished your design.

Left: Ceramic paints are not very hard wearing so protect your design with a coat of ceramic varnish once the paints are dry.

TECHNIQUES

As well as using the designs in this book, copy and adapt ones you see around, you, in books and magazines, shops, museums and art galleries. As you gain confidence begin to create your own designs — start with simple motifs, which can be extremely effective.

Designs will usually need adapting for your purpose — perhaps being simplified a little from the original. They will often be too small or too large for your purpose, but this is no problem — use a method known as squaring up to alter the size. This is the same method you will need to employ when using the templates in the back of this book. First cover the design with a grid of squares, either by drawing directly over it, or by copying the design onto tracing paper and then onto graph paper marked in 10mm (½in) squares. Now draw a second grid onto tracing paper. Make the squares larger to enlarge the original design, smaller to reduce it. For example, if the finished image is to be twice the size, make each square twice as large. Finally copy the design, one square at a time, onto the new grid, being careful to note where the design enters and leaves each of the squares.

To transfer a squared-up design to an object to be decorated turn the trace over and redraw the outline on the reverse side with a soft pencil. Then position the trace reverse side down on the object and go over the outline with a harder pencil or ballpoint pen. Alternatively place a sheet of carbon paper, carbon side down, between the tracing and the object, and redraw the outline as before.

China and glass do not take lead pencil well; use a waxy Chinagraph pencil (light or dark coloured as appropriate) to reinforce a traced outline, or if possible work freehand. Use a fabric pencil on fabrics.

Flower and leaf designs can easily be painted straight onto the object using pointed artists' brushes of varying sizes. Practise on paper, laying the brush down and seeing the shapes it produces. Use the tip of the brush to make dots.

When a design is completely symmetrical you only need to copy half of it. Draw a line exactly across the centre and reposition the trace to complete the design.

If you wish to enlarge a design, first draw a grid of squares over it. Now, using a set-square, draw an enlarged grid on a piece of plain white paper.

Copy the design on to the new grid, square by square, paying particular attention to where the design lines enter and leave the squares.

STENCILLING

The materials for stencilling are many and varied. Some projects only require one brush, one pot of stencil paint, a knife and a small sheet of acetate, so the cost need not be daunting.

There is a wide variety of paints suitable. Quick drying stencil paints are ideal. They are water-based for easy cleaning, and come in a wide range of colours. Stencil crayons are large oil-based crayons that produce a soft effect when applied with a stencil brush. They are very easy for a beginner as there is no danger of running paint leaking under the stencil. You can also use a number of water-based fabric paints. These are either of a jelly or fairly liquid consistency and are easy to apply with a stencil brush or sponge.

Other suitable paints include ordinary household emulsion paints, cellulose car spray paints and household spray paints. Acrylic paints are also good for flexible surfaces such as roller blinds or shower curtains.

The stencil itself can be made from anything which masks out an area of background. Although you can employ doilies, lace or even, masking tape to create a stencil effect, the most common stencil is one which is cut from a resilient type of cardboard or acetate.

Stencil card is brown, flexible, oiled cardboard that is very easy to cut, but opaque. This means you have to transfer the design directly on to it and that you cannot see through it to match up the design when stencilling. Plastic film sold for use in drawing offices, is very economical if you are going to do a lot of stencil cutting: a medium thickness film is best. All of these plastic films are transparent, which means you can lay the film over a design and cut straight through. You can also see through while stencilling, which is a great help when lining up a set of stencils.

To cut the stencil you will need a good craft knife with a replaceable blade. A rubberized self-healing cutting mat is the perfect base for cutting on, otherwise a sheet of thick cardboard makes a good substitute. To mark the film or card, you will need a thin waterproof felt-tipped pen. Low-tack masking tape is also essential for attaching the stencil to the wall or object without damaging the surface.

Remember, you will require a separate stencil for each colour being used so trace that part of the design which is to be painted in the first colour then trace the remainder of the design with a dotted line. Make a second and if necessary third stencil for subsequent colours. Now simply cut out the continuous line on each of the stencils using a stencil knife. Cut towards you, turning the stencil rather than the knife. On a repeating stencil pattern, such as a border, always draw a small part of the pattern either side of the main design so that you can use this for repositioning the stencil each time you finish a section.

Brush stencilling on hard surfaces is the traditional method of stencilling, producing the familiar speckled texture. Use a good quality, flat, or slightly domed, stencil brush. Pour a little paint into an old saucer and dip just the tips of the bristles into it. Dab off some of the excess paint on to a piece of kitchen paper and you are ready to stencil. Tape the design in place and, holding the brush upright, dab on the paint with a gentle 'bouncing' movement. Make sure the edge of the stencil area is coloured to maintain the outline of each shape, but you can leave the centre of each area very pale. Don't put on a thick layer of paint but build up the colours in certain areas to look like shadows, giving your design a three-dimensional quality. Check your progress by lifting the stencil occasionally and you'll find it is surprising how little paint you need to hold the design.

PAPER CRAFTS

Paper is a remarkably versatile material that comes in a vast and glorious range of types, from plain matt sheets to glossy gummed squares, from gossamer-thin tissue and delicate iridescent film to exquisitely patterned giftwrap. All these are made in dozens of beautiful colours, and there are also textured, flocked and metallic papers to add yet another dimension.

MATERIALS

Many types of paper are readily available from stationers, department stores and artists' materials shops, at no great cost. Crepe paper can be used almost like fabric as it stretches — when cut across the grain, the cut edge can be gently stretched to give an attractive fluted edge. Marbled paper, traditionally used as endpapers for hardbacked books, is particularly attractive, and if you make your own, every piece is unique.

In addition you can make good use of Victorian floral transfers, decorative sticky tapes, giftwrapping ribbons and even pieces of left over wallpaper or wallpaper borders. Keep every scrap of decorative paper that comes your way — paper doilies, greetings cards, pictures from magazines. Even the smallest bit can be put to good use.

The most useful type of cardboard for craft work is thin and

A wide range of different coloured and textured papers is available from art and craft shops, and the choice can be increased one hundred-fold if you also consider using wrapping paper or wallpaper for your designs. Giftwrapping ribbons, adhesive tapes, pipecleaners and pom-poms also come in a variety of bright colours and help add the finishing touches.

lightweight — roughly the same thickness as that used for cereal packet — although some projects call for sturdier, more constructional stuff. Decorative card, with a shiny, metallic or textured coating on one side, also has great possibilities — it is particularly good for making party hats and masks. Mounting board, made in multi layers and various thicknesses, is best for items that will be handled a lot.

For most papercraft use white PVA adhesive — the kind children use in school — which is easy to apply and can be washed off the hands with water. It does not stain and is non-toxic. As it dries to a clear glossy finish it can also be used as a protective varnish.

For a really professional finish use spray adhesive, which is expensive but has the great advantage that sprayed paper can be repositioned if you make a mistake. For extra strength — say when sticking card to wood — use woodworking or clear adhesives.

Other useful items include clear sticky tape, both single and double sided. Ordinary sticky tape becomes yellow and brittle with age, but another type, known as magic or invisible tape, is longer-lasting and stays clear, though it does not adhere quite so firmly.

Masking tape is handy for holding paper and cardboard in place while you work, as it is very low tack and does not tear the paper or leave a mark when removed.

TECHNIQUES

Success in papercraft depends on working very precisely. Be sure to work on a clean, completely flat surface, and wipe off any adhesive that gets on it as you go along. Use a small pair of sharp-pointed scissors for cutting paper and thin card. For thicker cardboard use a craft knife rather than a large pair of scissors — it gives a better finish. Replace the blades frequently as they soon become blunt. Always cut on a cutting mat, either purpose-made or improvised from corrugated cardboard. Cut straight lines against a steel rule, holding it down firmly with one hand and keeping fingers well away from the knife. When cutting thick cardboard make several cuts, going deeper each time; do not try to get right through in one stroke. To fold cardboard accurately score the fold lines lightly first, being careful not to cut too deep.

An HB (medium soft) pencil is the most versatile, but have a softer lead such as a 2B for sketching and going over the back of tracings. Keep all pencils sharpened to a fine point so that your drawing is accurate. Use a ruler for drawing straight lines, and a set square for drawing squares and rectangles so that the angles are perfectly correct. A compass is essential for drawing circles to exact sizes; for tiny ones a plastic stencil is handy.

Always use the correct adhesive for the job and follow the manufacturer's instructions carefully, testing it on scrap paper first. When using thin papers, use adhesive sparingly to make sure it does not seep through. Avoid getting it on the surface of printed papers, as the pattern may smudge. Use a plastic spreader or strip of cardboard to apply adhesive evenly over a flat surface.

Take special care when using spray adhesive. Protect the surrounding work surface with newspaper — or put the paper in a box. Spray an even film over the surface, then stick in place. Clean up any tacky areas with lighter fuel. Always choose an ozone-friendly spray, and be sure to work in a well ventilated room.

To make narrow giftwrapping ribbon curl, pull it smoothly over the blade of a pair of scissors.

Here are just some of the things you will find useful when working with paper. They include a cutting mat, set square, steel rule, compass, craft knife and scissors, plus a range of pencils, pens, glues and tapes.

FLOWER CRAFTS

The flowers used for flowercraft can be fresh, dried or ones made from silk or paper. The dried flowers used in this book include most of the readily available ones such as roses, achilles, gypsophila and lavender.

MATERIALS

A strong pair of scissors is essential, plus a pair of wire cutters or pliers. Secateurs (pruning shears) are useful for woody stems.

For supporting dried flower work buy dry foam, which comes in blocks, balls, drums and cone shapes. These can be secured to the container with plastic pinholders and fixative tape. Occasionally you will need cellulose filler to make up a heavy base. Fresh flowers can be supported with ordinary water-absorbent florists' foam. Crumpled wire mesh is a handy support for large arrangements.

To make wreaths, buy the basic circle of twisted twigs from a florists'; or make your own from bendy twigs such as birch.

Various types of wire are essential to dried flower work. Stub wires are straight lengths of wire in various thicknesses, generally used for supporting single flowerheads or binding together small groups of flowers. Black reel wire is used for making moss wreaths and garlands, which require a continuous length to bind the flowers and leaves in place. For more delicate work such as binding dried flowers into posies or wiring ribbon bows use reels or lengths of fine silver florists' wire.

Other useful items are florists' tape, for binding up bunches of flowers; some clear glue suitable for use with polystyrene for gluing foam to a container; also florists' fixative putty and adhesive pads, for general securing jobs. A hot glue gun easy to use, and provides a firm fixing.

TECHNIQUES

Some dried flowers, such as helichrysums, have weak stems that need supporting. Cut a stem down to about 4cm (1½in) and place it against one end of a stub wire. Bind the length of the stem to the wire using silver reel wire. This method can also be used to lengthen too-short flower stems; if they are hollow, simply push the stub wire inside to add extra support and give the arrangement stability.

To give flowers more impact in a display, wire them into small bunches before arranging them. First bend the end of a stub wire to form a hair-pin shape.

Cut the flower stems short and place them against the pin. Wind the long end of wire round about three times then straighten it to make a 'stem'.

Bows are often used to put the finishing touches to an arrangement. To make this double bow, take a length of satin ribbon about 60cm (2ft) long and make a loop at one end. Form a second loop as shown to make a bow shape. Ensure each time you loop the ribbon that you keep it right side out.

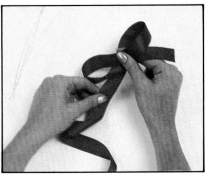

Loop the long tail over the front of the bow to form a third loop, and then to the back to make a fourth loop as shown.

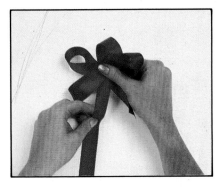

Wrap a length of rose wire round the centre of the bow and secure it by twisting the ends together. Use the ends of the wire to attach the bow to the arrangement. Now simply trim the tails to the required length, cutting them in a V-shape to finish off. This technique can easily be adapted to make a single bow or even a triple or quadruple one.

INTERIOR DESIGN

In this chapter we explore decorative painting techniques such as stippling, sponging and ragging shown here, though these need not simply be applied to walls. Remember, each technique can be applied to different objects and often different surfaces. So experiment a little! We also show just how versatile the art of stencilling can be. Again, walls are not the only option — you can stencil curtains, cushions and even lampshades to echo the theme of stencilled walls. Look at pages 12 through to 16 for inspiration.

Stippling is a paint technique which gives an attractive soft finish, made up with a myriad of tiny dots of colour. The wall below is stippled with emulsion paint in two shades of blue — forget-me-not and moon shadow — on a lavender white base. Begin by applying the base colour with a roller or brush, giving two coats if necessary.

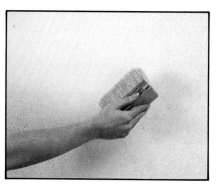

Stippling brushes are wide with a large number of bristles and, traditionally made from badger hair, they are quite expensive to buy. As an alternative you could try using a brush or broom. Lightly dip the brush into your paint so that only the very ends of the bristles are covered. Then apply the paint to the walls with a very light touch so as not to blur the image.

Evenly cover the wall with the first colour, trying not to overlap the stippling. Wash your brush and leave it to dry before applying the second colour as before. Fill in any spaces and overlap the previously stippled areas. Before you take on a whole room, experiment on one small area first to perfect your technique.

RAGGING

There are two main methods of ragging: 'ragging off', in which you apply rags to a wet wall of paint, so removing the colour and leaving a pattern; or 'ragging on' as shown here. In the latter, the colour is applied with bunched-up rags, in a similar way to sponging. First apply a base coat of emulsion paint with a roller or a brush.

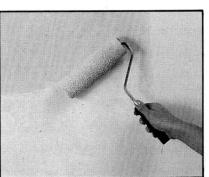

Use dry rags for this technique — it is the crisp folds in the fabric that form the pattern. Make sure you cut up lots of rags before you start and have plenty of waste paper around. Clasp a rag in your hand and dip it lightly into the paint. Dab off the top layer of paint on to some waste paper, then apply the cloth to the wall with a dabbing motion.

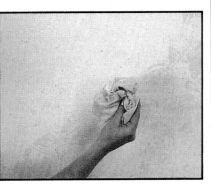

Continue to apply paint in a random pattern, replacing the rag with a fresh one as soon as it becomes too damp. When the first colour has dried, apply a second colour as before: a contrasting colour can look particularly effective.

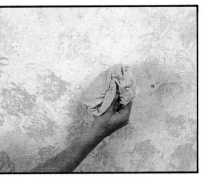

SPONGING

Sponging is one of the easiest paint finishes to achieve. You can use one, two or more colours. When choosing colours, go for a light, mid and darker shade of the same colour. Here, rose white has been used as a base for soft peach and dusky apricot. It is a good idea to buy some small samples of emulsion paint to practise with before you start. First, apply the base coat with a brush or roller.

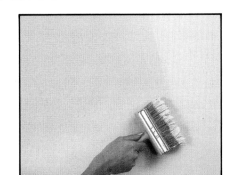

When your base colour is dry, take a natural sponge and dampen it. Now dip the sponge into the second colour, being careful not to overload it with paint. Remove any excess paint by dabbing the sponge on to waste paper, then apply paint to the walls with a light dabbing motion. Don't press hard or the paint will smudge. Continue in a random pattern, re-applying paint to the sponge as necessary.

Wash out your sponge and apply the third colour, overlapping the second colour. When you have finished you should have an even blending of the three colours. If the last colour is too dominant you can soften it by sponging over with some of the base colour.

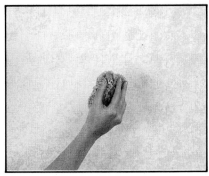

GARDEN ROOM

This lovely light sitting-room looked rather bare with plain walls, despite the number of pictures decorating it. To give it an outdoor feel, a trellis design has been stencilled in panels just below the coving. These panels give a definite area within which to hang the pictures, making the most of the pictures visually.

The wisteria design is stencilled in a random fashion over the trellis so that you can 'grow' as many flowers as you like. On page 90 there's one stencil design for the large blossom and one for the smaller spray with accompanying leaves and buds. By using all or part of these and turning the stencils over, you can create an infinite variety of groups of flowers. Very natural colours are used here to mimic the real garden shades but you could just as well stencil the leaves in grey and the blooms in shades of pink and peach to match existing furniture and drapes. Alternatively, you could paint the flowers pale yellow suggesting a laburnum tree rather than wisteria.

The accessories such as the curtains, lamp and cushions have all been stencilled to complement the trellis design and make the room feel part of one whole theme, using colours and styles to bring it all together .

WISTERIA TRELLIS BORDER

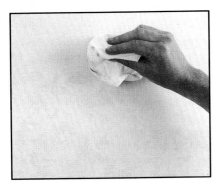

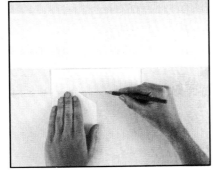

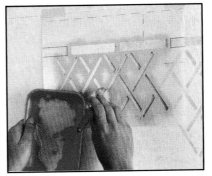

First paint the walls in a cool minty green. The subtle texture of ragging looks very effective with stencilling. To achieve this effect, pour a little creamy yellow emulsion paint into an old dish and dip a scrunched up square of rag into it. Blot the excess on to spare paper and then dab the rag on to the wall in a random fashion to create an open texture.

Measure a little way down from the coving or ceiling and cut a cardboard template to mark this distance around the room as shown. This will help you align the top of the stencil. Enlarge the stencil designs on pages 90 and 91 using the squaring up method. Next cut the stencils: two end trellis pieces and one joining piece; one large and one small wisteria stencil; and one leaf stencil.

Start by taping the two end trellis stencils on to the wall and then mark where the joining piece will go, adjusting the ends to fit the design exactly. Mark lightly in pencil. Begin stencilling at one end using quick-drying stencil paints. Stencil very lightly in pale grey and accentuate the colour where the struts go under each other to look like a shadow and give a 3-D effect.

Position the wisteria and leaf stencils randomly to make large and small bunches. Start at a corner and work towards the trellis centre, waiting for the paint to dry before you overlap the next stencil. Mix the colours so that you get a varied range from blue to mauve in the flowers and several shades of green leaves. Clean the stencil with a damp cloth to use the reverse side.

TRELLIS PELMET

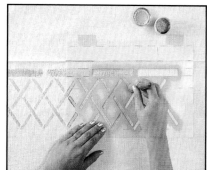

T he pelmet is made of stiffened calico to match the curtain fabric. You need a piece of calico about 56cm (22in) wide, and 60cm (24in) longer than your window. Fold the fabric in half along the length and stencil the joining trellis motif 2cm (¾in) down from the fold. Use grey fabric paint, dabbing it on lightly with a stencil brush for a speckled texture.

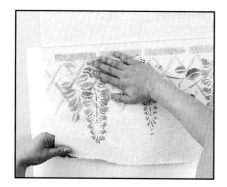

Stencil the flowers and leaves, keeping below the fold line. Leave to dry and then iron to fix the fabric paint. Cut a piece of self-adhesive pelmet stiffening about 5cm (2in) shorter than the stencilled fabric. Peel off the backing paper and press the fabric on to the stiffening, making the top edge of the stiffening run along the fold. Smooth out any air bubbles.

Peel the backing paper off the reverse side and press the fabric on to the back. Turn in the ends to neaten. Draw a line just below the trellis and then cut along this and around the flowers. Fix a strip of Velcro along the reverse side of the top edge and attach the matching half of the Velcro to a pelmet rail positioned so that the trellis on the pelmet lines up with the wall border. Press in place.

WISTERIA TABLE LAMP

U se the flower and leaf stencils to decorate a plain coolie lampshade to go with your wisteria trellis room. Start with a spray of leaves and then add the flower spray. Work around the shade to make a balanced pattern. Use fabric paints and stencil very lightly so that the light will shine through and bring out the colours rather than making a dark silhouette.

Decorate the pottery lamp base too using the curtain border motif. Tape the stencil carefully around the lamp so that it does not slip. Stencil lightly with peach coloured ceramic paint. Leave to dry, then shade with a light coat of mauve paint. Adjust the border stencil so that it meets up around the lamp without leaving a gap. Leave to dry for 24 hours, then varnish to complete.

The hese cream silk cushions are stencilled in metallic fabric paints and quilted to make sumptuous accessories. Draw up and cut out the quarter design stencils from page 15. Mark the horizontal and vertical lines on the stencil and match these up with central pressed folds on a 48cm (19in) square of cream Honan silk. Tape the silk in place on a worktop protected with paper.

Tape the stencil in position and dip the brush into pearl, gold or silver lustre. Wipe off the excess and dip into gold powder. Shake off any excess and stencil with a light dabbing stroke. Move the stencil around the silk, lining up the marks with the creases·in the silk each time to complete the pattern. Leave the paint to dry for about 24 hours, then set with a hot iron.

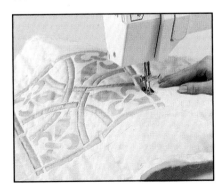

Cut a piece of polyester wadding the same size as the silk. Tack the layers together with several rows of stitching to hold securely in place. Using a sewing machine, stitch around some or all of the stencilled motifs to quilt them. Pull all the threads to the back, tie and cut off. Cut two backing pieces of silk 25cm x 48cm (10in x 19in). Turn under one long edge on each piece.

With right sides together and raw edges matching, pin and stitch the two backing pieces to the cushion front. Trim the wadding from the 1.5cm (⅝in) seam allowance and turn the cover right side out. Press lightly. Stitch parallel rows around the cover through all the layers to make a 6cm (2½in) wide border. Insert a 30cm (12in) cushion pad and hand stitch the opening.

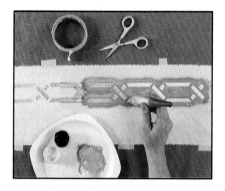

Trace and cut out the border stencil opposite to make a decorative padded edging for plain calico curtains. Cut a piece of calico 25cm (10in) wide and the length of each curtain. Tape the fabric flat on the work surface and lightly stencil in mauve to match the wisteria stencil. Place the stencil to print 4.5cm (1¾in) from one raw edge of the fabric.

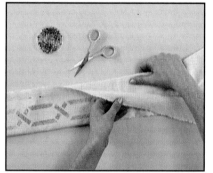

Leave the stencilled fabric to dry and then fix the paint with a hot iron. Fold the fabric in half lengthwise and lay a double thickness of curtain interlining or bump between the layers of calico. This should be the same width as the folded calico. Pin the top layer and the interlining together along the raw edge to hold in place.

Make up some piping using narrow cord and a bias strip of toning chintz or repp. Pin and stitch this to the top layer of calico and the interlining. Pin this, right sides together, along the leading edge of your curtain and stitch close to the piping cord. Fold the free edge of the border to the reverse side of the curtain, turn in the raw edge and slipstitch to finish.

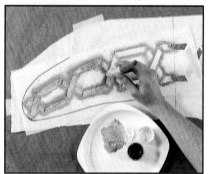

Enlarge and cut out the tie-back stencil, marking the outline of the shape on the acetate. Mark a line halfway across the calico and stencil as for the curtain border, using fabric paints. Leave to dry and fix with a hot iron. Cut out a piece of pelmet stiffening to the tie-back shape, remove the backing and press on to the back of the stencilled calico.

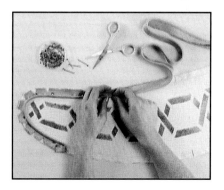

Trim the excess calico leaving 2cm (¾in) all around. Pin on covered piping cord, matching raw edges and clipping the curves. Stitch around the edge, close to the cord. Remove the other backing sheet and fold the seam allowance to the back. Cut another calico tie-back, press under the raw edge and slipstitch to back of the stencilled tie-back. Stitch a small ring to each end.

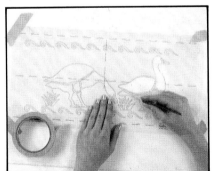

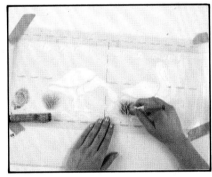

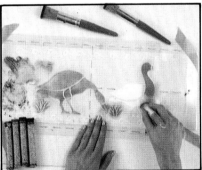

This stencil border is inspired by a 3rd century BC Egyptian painting. First, draw the design on page 93 to the required size, referring to the instructions on squaring up on page 7. With masking tape, attach some stencil film over the design and cut out the shapes using a stencil or craft knife.

You can stencil with either paint or crayons. Stencil crayons have been used here as they give a soft effect, similar to spraying. Position the stencil over your border and tape it in place. Now rub some crayon on to one corner of the stencil film and then dip the brush into the colour. Apply the colour to the area you wish to stencil using a circular motion.

Lighter shades should be applied first, with dark tones added on top to provide shading and depth of colour. It is a good idea to use a separate brush for each colour so that you do not get a muddy effect.

To finish the stencil, colour in the border design in a slightly stronger terracotta colour. Draw the eyes on to the geese using a pencil. When you have finished one section of the border, move the stencil along to the next area and repeat the process. Once you are confident at stencilling, as an alternative to painting a border, you can paint straight on to the wall.

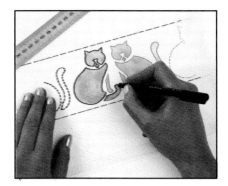

Brighten your bedroom with a charming border of fat felines. Referring to the design shown opposite, cut out an acetate stencil sheet, making it about 10cm (4in) larger all round than the motif. Use masking tape to hold the sheet in place centrally over the design and then carefully trace off the solid outlines and all the dotted guidelines using a waterproof felt-tip pen.

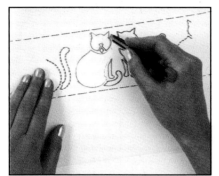

Place the acetate stencil sheet on a flat surface or cutting board and, using a craft knife, carefully cut out the design, following the solid outline. If you intend to use two or more colours in your border, as we have, you can make a separate stencil for each colour, cutting out only the relevant areas on each one.

Using a soft leaded pencil, lightly mark a base line or top line around your wall, measuring carefully to ensure that it runs parallel to your dado rail, picture rail, door frame or whatever. Attach the stencil in position with masking tape, lining up the dotted line with the pencil line on the wall.

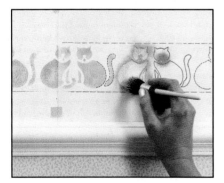

Pour a little stencil paint into a saucer. Dip the brush into the paint and dab it on to some dry kitchen paper. Test the brush on a scrap of paper and, when the paint stops looking blotchy, begin to work on the stencil using a light circular movement, going first in a clockwise and then in an anti-clockwise direction.

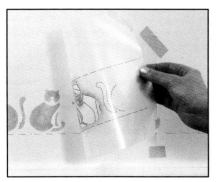

Lift the stencil away from the wall occasionally to check your progress. When all the shapes have been filled in to your satisfaction, carefully lift off the stencil and reposition it over the next area to be painted. Match the dotted lines over the previous stencil motif in order to keep the designs evenly spaced.

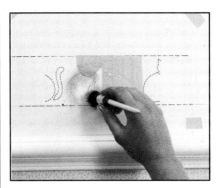

For a multi-coloured design, as an alternative to making several stencils you can use a single one and mask off unwanted areas with tape. Always finish one colour before you reposition the mask and begin to stencil the next colour, and remember to allow the paint to dry between coats to avoid smudging.

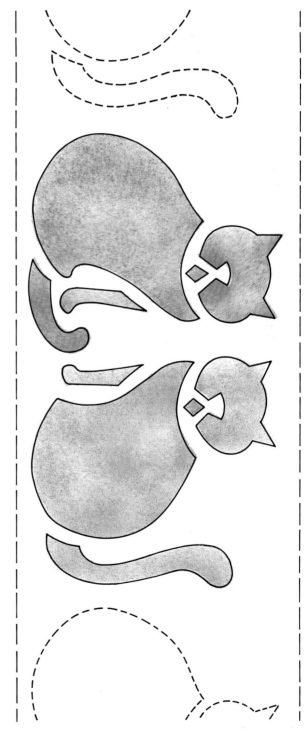

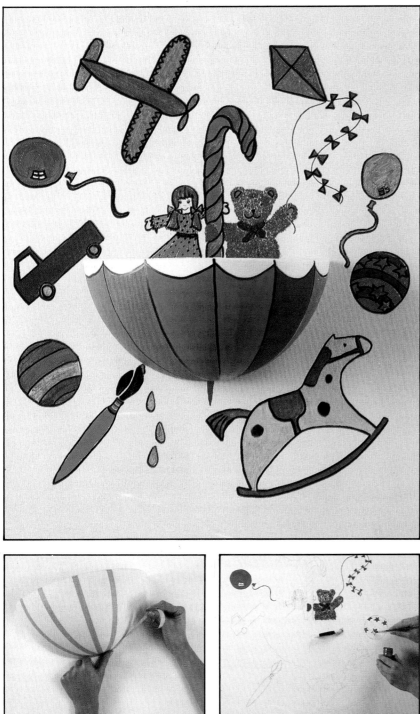

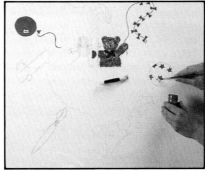

In this colourful design, a wall light is transformed into an umbrella bursting with toys. First mark the segments of the umbrella by putting strips of masking tape on to the shade as shown and ruling down one edge of each strip with a multi-purpose felt tip paint pen. Remove the tape and colour each segment using acrylic paints. Draw an outline of the shade on to the wall.

Draw the various elements of the design in pencil on to tracing paper — restrict your shapes to balloons, balls and kites if you are not too confident about more complex shapes. Pencil over the reverse of each trace and transfer the images on to the wall. As before, use acrylic paints to colour in the toys. Complete the picture by fixing the shade in position.

For those of you who like plants but lack green fingers, why not paint your own plant, cascading down from a wall lamp. Make an outline of your shade on to the wall so you know where to position the plant. Now, using a house plant as reference, draw the design on to the wall. Use a pencil so you can rub out any mistakes.

If you are using a translucent lightshade like this one, you can draw some of the leaves within the outline so that they show through the shade. Paint the leaves using acrylic paints or even artist's oils, though the latter will take a little longer to dry. Use dark colours to create shadow and depth, and light colours to add highlights. Finally, fix your shade in place. As you can see, the effect is stunning.

TUTTI-FRUTTI TILES

Handpainted tiles are expensive to buy, but it's easy to create your own using plain tiles and a stencilled pattern. The fruit motifs used here are most suitable for a kitchen, but several of the other design templates included in the back of the book could be adapted for use in other locations such as bathrooms or tiled splashbacks in bedrooms.

Ceramic paint is the easiest to use, being water based, but as it is not terribly hardwearing it must be protected when dry with a coat of ceramic varnish. For a tougher finish use solvent-based enamel paints instead. Clean the tiles with washing-up liquid or non-scratch cleaner rather than harsh abrasives to avoid damaging the design.

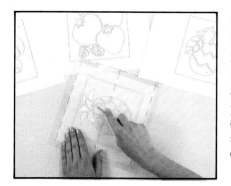

Stencilled tiles really brighten up a kitchen, and you can complete a project like this in a day. Either square up the designs provided in the back of the book (as described on page 7) or draw your own design on to tracing paper. Using masking tape, attach the design to a cutting board. Tape the stencil film on top of the design and cut it out using a stencil knife.

Before you begin painting, wash and dry the tiles to make sure they are free from dirt and grease. Attach the cut stencil to a tile with masking tape. Pour some ceramic paint on to a saucer and dip the stencil brush into it. Dab off any surplus paint on to waste paper, then apply the colour to the required area of the stencil. Start with the lightest colour, then apply the darker tones on top.

Add subsequent colours to other areas of the stencil, again starting with the lightest and building up texture and shade with each application. Wait for the paint to dry before removing the stencil. Then carefully clean up any smudged areas with a craft knife or a paint brush dipped in turpentine. Finally, protect the design with a coat of ceramic varnish.

DECORATED FURNITURE

U se paint to give old furniture a brand new look or to brighten up very plain modern pieces. Before investing time and effort in renovating old wooden furniture make sure it is free of woodworm, indicated by a scattering of small neat holes. If any are present, treat by injecting woodworm fluid into them — leave to dry thoroughly before painting as the fluid is oily. Also do any necessary repairs and remove any dangerous splinters or old nails, especially if the piece is to be used by children. Old paint can be left on if it is in reasonable condition — just sand down with fine abrasive paper to 'key' the surface. But badly chipped paint should all be stripped off.

PRETTY PASTEL COT

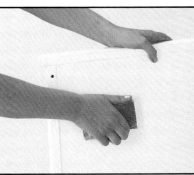

N ew cots can be expensive, so why not give an old one a face lift with a new coat of paint? But rather than simply painting it all one colour, use a range of pretty pastel shades to create a stylish effect. Before you begin painting, dismantle the cot and replace any loose bars with dowelling of the required diameter. Then sand the old surface down so it is smooth. Dust well before painting.

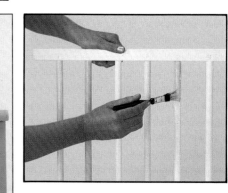

If necessary, give the cot a coat of undercoat. In pencil, number each bar according to the colour you intend to paint it — in this case the numbers one to three represent pink, yellow and blue respectively. Using lead free nursery paint, colour the bars according to the numbers, finishing one colour before cleaning the brush and starting the next. Apply a second coat if necessary once the first has dried.

Using the same three paints, paint the inside of the cot ends in one colour and the outside in another. Now choose a fourth, stronger shade to paint the surrounds on both the ends and sides of the cot. Apply a second coat as necessary.

LEAFY MIRROR FRAME

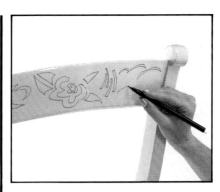

A vine leaf design is used to enhance a plain mirror frame. The design can be painted with acrylic or a combination of ceramic and glass paints, using different shades of green, plus brown, white, yellow and black. Protect the glass before you start painting with a layer of paper stuck down around the edges with masking tape.

To age the frame, stain it with brown and green glass paint diluted with turpentine. When the stain is dry, finish with a coat of varnish. Another way of ageing the frame is to give it a coat of crackle varnish.

BLOOMSBURY CHAIR

This chair was inspired by designs of the 'Bloomsbury Group' (a London-based group of artists and writers). First, give a plain wooden chair a fresh coat of gloss paint. Then, referring to the pattern in the main photograph, draw the design on to the surface using a fine black felt tip pen.

Using gloss paints, colour in the design with a fine brush, making sure you just cover the black outlines so that the design remains soft, rather than hard-edged.

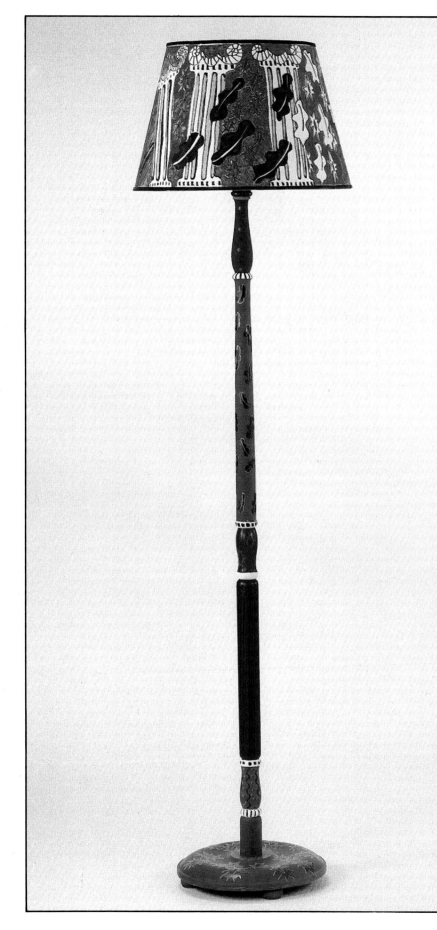

Here's something for those who enjoy the outrageous and the avant garde — an old standard lamp eye-catchingly decorated with Doric columns and oak leaves. Following the maker's instructions, strip the original finish off the lamp-stand with varnish remover. Use an old toothbrush to get into difficult corners. Rub down the surface with wire wool then sand it to give a smooth finish.

Paint the stand with primer and, when this is dry, apply some undercoat. Alternatively, you could use two coats of combined primer/undercoat. Leave the stand to dry before you begin to apply the colour.

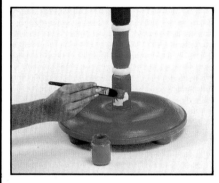

Decorate the standard lamp with acrylic paints, using bold, primary colours. Paint different parts of the lamp different colours, and break the colours up with rings of white, using the carved features as guidelines.

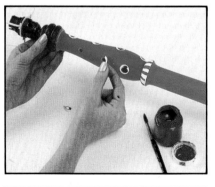

Now decorate the base colours with dots, dashes, spots, leaves and columns, using both acrylic paints and multi-purpose felt tip paint pens. Paint the spots by sticking ring reinforcements on to one section of the stand and filling in the holes with a brightly contrasting colour. Paint black oak leaves on another section and outline them in bright yellow using the felt tip pens.

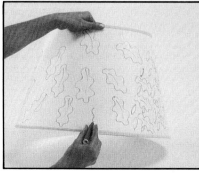

When the stand is dry, apply a coat of protective varnish. Outline your design on the shade with a fine line fabric felt tip pen, repeating the patterns used on the stand. Now fill in the design with thick fabric pens, continuing to use brightly contrasting colours.

MARBLED PLANT STAND

Turn a plain wooden pedestal into a stunning marbled plant stand. Stands such as these are available from craft suppliers (look in craft magazines for stockists). Successful marbling requires a lot of practice, so experiment on a spare piece of wood before tackling the real thing. Prime and undercoat the surface as necessary, then apply a coat of black eggshell paint.

Now mix a white tinted glaze using 60% scumble (available from decorating shops) to 20% white eggshell paint and 20% white spirit. Dab the glaze on to the surface with a decorator's brush, allowing plenty of the black to show through.

Rag over the wet glaze with a soft cloth, spreading the glaze to give a dappled effect, and still making sure some of the black shows through. Soften the ragging effect with a stippling brush and a rag dipped in white spirit.

Mix a small quantity of black glaze using the same proportions as before: 60% scumble; 20% black eggshell paint; 20% white spirit. Now use a fine pointed brush to paint on the black veining.

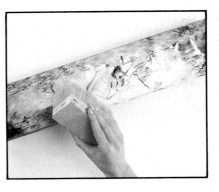

As you finish veining an area, soften the effect with a stippling brush to break up the hard edges. When you have completed the black veining, repeat the process with white glaze, using a stippling brush to soften the edges as before. When the paint is dry, apply a coat of polyurethane varnish to give the glossy cold sheen of marble.

SPONGED CABINET

An old piece of utility furniture, long past its prime, is transformed with a beautiful paint finish and some new china handles. Choose a light coloured emulsion paint for the base colour, plus a medium and a dark shade for the sponging on. Before you start to redecorate, you will need to remove the old finish.

Place the piece of furniture in a well ventilated room, standing it on plenty of newspaper to protect the surrounding floor. Apply paint stripper according to the manufacturer's instructions; leave for the required length of time and then scrape off the old paint. Wash down the surface with liquid detergent and water and, when dry, sand it until the wood is smooth.

Next, apply a primer, an undercoat and then an emulsion base colour, leaving the cupboard to dry between coats. Take a natural sponge, wet it and squeeze it so it is just damp. Dip it into your second colour and dab any excess paint on to waste paper before applying paint to the cupboard. Use a light dabbing motion so that you do not smudge the paint, and leave lots of gaps for the next colour.

Apply the third and darkest colour with a clean sponge, filling in any gaps and overlapping other sponged areas.

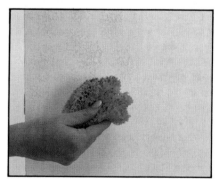

Finally, using ceramic paint, decorate some plain white china handles with a pretty leaf or floral pattern. If you need inspiration for your design, try looking at an old china cup or plate.

FLORAL LLOYD LOOM

In recent years, Lloyd loom chairs such as this have become collectors' items. But because so many of them are now in poor condition, they are often renovated and painted with an attractive motif. The flamboyance of this design is intended to reflect the warm sunny conservatory for which such chairs were originally intended.

You can either paint the chair using aerosol spray paint or apply paint in the traditional manner with a paint brush. Draw your rose design on to the chair, using a soft pencil and keeping the flowers big and bold. Colour in the design with acrylic paints, mixing the colours to get a wide range of shades. Use dark shades to add shadow and depth, and lighter shades for the highlights.

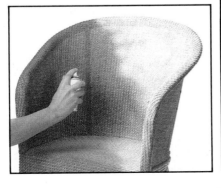

BAMBOO STOOL

Bambooing is a simple but effective paint technique which can add interest to a plain piece of cane furniture. Before you start to paint, remove any varnish from your furniture with varnish remover. Dilute some brown acrylic paint with water to make a wash, then, using a 20mm (¾in) brush, paint bands of colour at intervals along the cane.

Next, using the same colour undiluted and a fine brush, paint on the markings. First, paint lines of colour in the centre of the band of wash. Next paint elongated 'V' shapes in pairs at right angles to the lines, finishing off with tiny dots by the sides of the Vs. When the bambooing is complete, apply a coat of varnish to protect the paintwork.

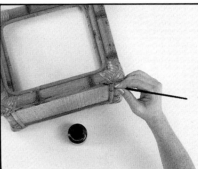

A striking 'Mondrian' inspired design in bold colours gives a new lease of life to a battered old director's chair. Even if you don't have an old chair to do up it's still worth buying a new one to customize. As well as paint brushes masking tape and a sponge, you will also require varnish, acrylic paints, opaque fabric paints and a black fabric paint pen.

Remove the canvas from your chair; if it is old, you can replace it later with new deck chair canvas. Sand down the chair frame until the wood is smooth and fill any cracks with wood filler. Now paint the outline of the frame with black acrylic paint, applying a second coat if necessary.

Using red, green and blue acrylic paint and a fine paint brush, paint the cross pieces, the central dowels and the ends of the legs and arms in alternating bright colours. Acrylic paints dry very quickly so clean your brush instantly between each colour.

When the paint is completely dry, give the frame a couple of coats of varnish to protect it. Leave the first coat to dry before applying the second one.

Using either the original covers or some new fabric cut to size, put strips of masking tape across the canvas, masking off a series of rectangles both large and small. Rub the tape down with the back of a spoon to give it extra adhesion.

Pour some opaque fabric paint into a saucer and dip a sponge into the colour. Dab the paint on to a masked area of the canvas being sure not to get any paint on the adjacent squares. Use a sponge rather than a paint brush to avoid brush strokes. When you have finished applying one colour, take a clean sponge and apply the next. Continue like this until all the rectangles are filled in.

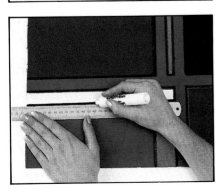

You may find you have to use more than one coat of paint if you are working on a very dark background. When the paint is completely dry, tear off all the masking tape. Finish by drawing a black rule round each of the rectangles, using a fabric paint pen. You can now put the canvas back on the chair.

Here's a cheerful way to decorate some inexpensive plastic chairs for a party or kid's playroom. All you need are some fine multi-purpose felt tip pens and a chinagraph pencil. Using the chinagraph pencil, draw your design on to the seat and the back of the chair, creating bold shapes and patterns. Rub out any mistakes with a soft cloth soaked in lighter fuel.

Colour in your outlines with the multi-purpose pens, using brightly contrasting and even clashing colours. Decorate the stars with dots, spots, dashes and triangles of black.

Outline the edges of the shapes in black to make the images sharper. Finally, link up the various elements of your design with colourful streamers and more dots and dashes.

Personalize a pine toy chest with your child's name and a delightful array of wild animals. You will find a template of the design on page 93; all you have to do is add the name. Using wire wool and white spirit, remove any wax finish from the box. Wipe the chest down with clean soapy water and, when dry, sand down any rough edges.

Draw the design on to tracing paper, then go over the back of the trace with a pencil. Now tape the design on to the box and trace over the original line. This will only leave a faint mark unless the wood is new, so go over the lines with a pencil or even a fine felt tip pen.

Using acrylic paints, start painting in the design. An old plate or saucer will serve as a palette on which to mix your paints. Try to add tonal variation with light and dark shades, but if you are not happy doing this, keep the colours flat.

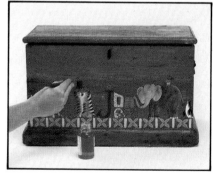

When the paint is dry you can strengthen the outlines by drawing round them once more with a pencil or fine felt tip pen. Use a pen or pencil to add fine details such as whiskers, eyes and mouths as well. Finally, give the box a coat of clear varnish. This will not only protect the design but will also make the colours come to life.

An old chest of drawers is stripped down and given new life with a beautiful rose motif. The idea works just as effectively on modern pine furniture. If necessary, strip off the old finish with varnish remover or paint stripper, according to the manufacturer's instructions. Use an old toothbrush to get into difficult corners. Rub the wood down with wire wool and then sand it until it is smooth.

Draw the design on to tracing paper, referring to the template on page 92. Draw variations on this design for the back plate and centre drawer. Either trace the design on to the furniture or cut it out and draw round the shape, filling in the detail afterwards.

Start to paint the design with acrylic paints, mixing the colours well so that you have a wide range of shades and tones. Use darker shades to create shadow and depth, and light shades, including a touch of white, to add highlights.

When your design is finished and completely dry, apply a coat of varnish to the rose motifs. You can then wax the woodwork, applying several coats of beeswax polish to build up a good finish. Alternatively, you can save your energy by varnishing the entire chest.

FABRIC PAINTING

The popularity of fabric painting has grown rapidly in recent years. This is partly due to the many new materials on the market and the ease with which they can be applied; it also reflects people's desire to express their individuality. You will find in this chapter many different types of painted fabrics, from deckchair covers, blinds and curtains to cook's aprons, cushions and greetings cards. You can decorate fabrics with simple potato-cut prints or fabric felt tip pens, or even try your hand at the stunning art of silk painting (see page 39 for details). Some of the projects featured are very inexpensive, others are more costly, but all will prove worth the time, expense and effort entailed.

DEEP SEA DECK CHAIR

Here's a colourful way to transform an old deck chair. Remove the old canvas and fill any holes in the frame with wood filler. Sand down any rough wood until smooth. Apply a coat of primer, followed by one of undercoat, then finish with a brightly coloured gloss paint. Be sure to let each coat dry thoroughly before applying the next one.

You will need some new deck chair canvas to replace the old fabric, plus a white fabric pencil and some opaque fabric paints in a wide range of colours. First draw your design on to the canvas with the fabric pencil, referring to the template on page 94.

Paint the canvas using the opaque paints, cleaning your brush carefully between each colour. Paint the fish in bright colours and lively patterns; outline and segment the shells in gold and the star fish in bright orange. Iron the fabric on the back to fix the colours then tack the canvas on to the deck chair frame.

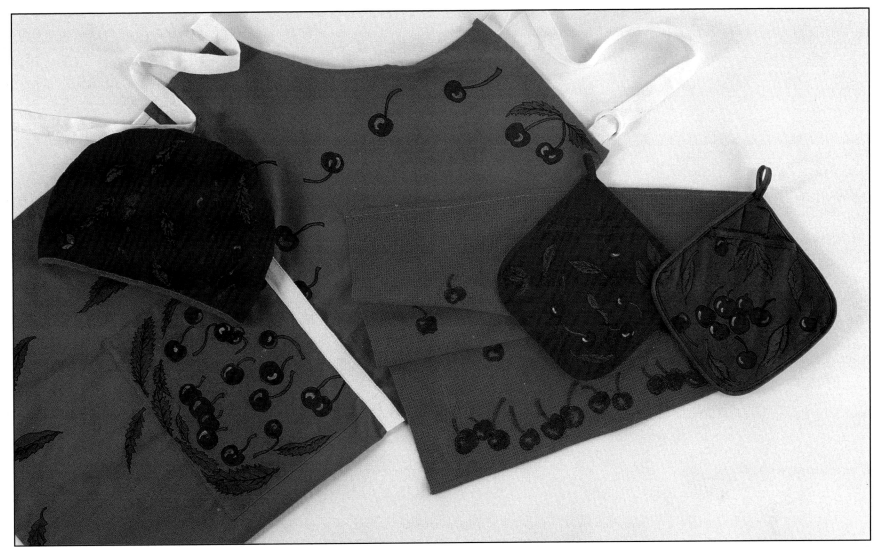

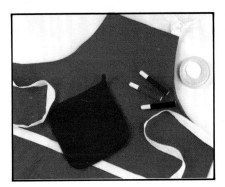

Co-ordinate your kitchen 'wear' with a simple but effective design of cherries. You will need some fabric felt tip pens and/or some opaque fabric paint plus an apron, tea cosy, pot holder and tea towel to decorate.

Practise the design on some paper first, then, when you are confident, use a fine fabric felt tip pen to draw the outline of your design on to the fabric. Here, the leaves and cherries have been spaced out so that they appear to be tumbling down from the tree. On the apron pocket the leaves are grouped to act as a nest for the falling cherries.

Now fill in the outlines with red and green paint. On dark backgrounds you will need to use opaque paints; these are harder to apply than the felt tip pens, so be patient and keep going over the design to achieve the intensity of colour desired.

When the paint is dry, use the black felt tip pen to add veins to the leaves and shading to the cherries. To complete the design, add white highlights to the cherries. This can be done either with a pen or with the opaque fabric paint. Finally, iron the back of the fabric to fix the paints.

A ROOM WITH A VIEW

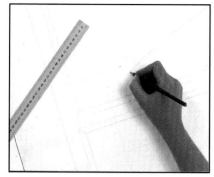

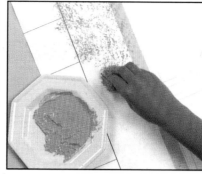

Create a beautiful landscape from your window using a range of paint techniques, from masking and sponging to potato cut printing. Size up the design opposite and lay your roller blind over it, holding it in place with masking tape. Lightly pencil in the main features such as the window frame, garden and cat.

Remove the tape holding the pattern, then mask off the outer edge of the window frame. Dab the surrounding area with a moist sponge dipped in paint.

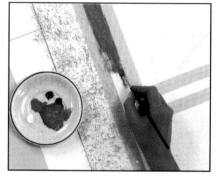

When the paint is dry, mask around the window frame. Mix some paints with acrylic medium to make the colour of stripped pine. Using a dry oil painting brush, paint the window frame, dragging the paint in lines to resemble wood grain. Next, mask around and paint other areas – such as the sky, hills and lake.

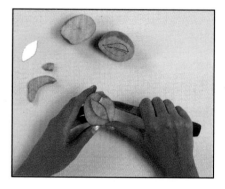

To print the foliage, first cut a potato in half and dry the surface. Using a cardboard template made from one of the leaf shapes shown opposite, trace a leaf on to the cut surface of the potato. Cut vertically into the potato, following this outline, then cut away the excess potato from the edges to leave a flat raised leaf shape.

Mask off the painted window frame with several widths of tape. Mix up a soft green colour and paint some on to the leaf shape, then press the potato cut on to the blind. Continue to print leaves, using a range of greens and overlapping the shapes to give a natural effect. Then use a fine brush to paint the leaf stems.

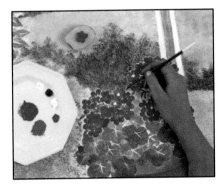

Make some geranium flower and leaf potato cuts in the same way and use them to print the geranium plant. Also paint a few buds and stems using a brush. When this is dry, mask and paint the pot in shades of terracotta using a larger brush. Finally, mask and paint the cat, finishing off with a fine set of whiskers.

Trace the leaves and flowers directly from the page and turn the shapes into cardboard templates.

One square represents 10cm (4in)

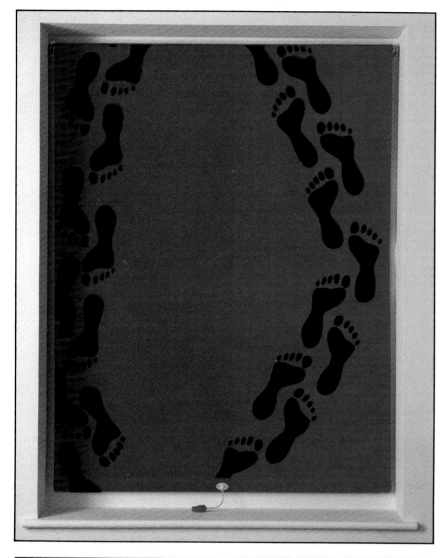

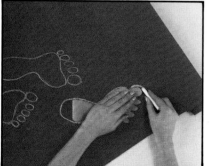

This is a very simple but effective design for a blind. All you need is a plain blind, some chalk, black fabric paint, a black fabric felt tip pen and your own two feet! Draw round your foot on tracing paper and cut out the shape. Use this as a template to draw feet on to the blind with chalk, drawing the toes individually as shown. Keep turning the template over to get left and right footprints.

When you have chalked your design going up and down the blind, draw over the chalk with a black fabric pen. Fill in the centre of each foot with black fabric paint then iron on the reverse side of the fabric to fix the colour.

Forget city life and make-believe you live in a cottage by the sea with this colourful blind. A photograph of a sea gull is a useful reference when drawing the bird. Create your design at a reasonable size first, then square it up to full size (see page 7) so that it fits on the blind. Draw the design on to a plain white blind in pencil.

When painting such a complex picture, it is a good idea to paint the background first, so start with the sky. This is a mixture of white and blue fabric paint, sponged on quite densely. The clouds are sponged on more lightly. Once the background is painted, start painting in the details. When you've finished, iron the back of the fabric to fix the paints.

CURTAINS A LA MODE

These attractive full-length curtains will add style to any modern living room and can be painted in any colour to match the decor. You will need lots of space when painting the fabric so cover your floor with plenty of newspaper before you begin. Now rip sheets and sheets of newspaper into long strips. It is best to use quality newspapers as they are wider and have more pages.

Sew together enough fabric to make a curtain and lay it out on the floor. Tape several strips of newspaper together so that they fit across the width of your fabric. Now, using loops of masking tape on the underside of the paper, stick the strips to the cloth, leaving gaps between the rows. As you work your way towards the top of the cloth, break up the rows with small 'islands' of paper.

Pour some opaque black fabric paint on to a saucer or plate and, starting at the bottom of the cloth, sponge the paint between the rows of newspaper.

With each new row, mix a little white opaque fabric paint into the black before you dip the sponge in. Keep adding white with each successive row so that the colour gradually changes from black to grey as you print up the cloth. By the time you get to the top where you have the islands of paper the colour should be light grey.

Leave the fabric paint to dry before removing the paper. Repeat the whole procedure with the second curtain. Iron on the back of each piece of fabric to fix the colour and then make them up into curtains.

POTATO PRINT CUSHIONS

Y ou probably think of potato printing as something you used to do in primary school — well think again! It can be used to great effect when decorating soft furnishings for the home. Cut a potato in half and draw the design on to one half with a felt tip pen. Now cut around the motif so that the design stands proud of the background.

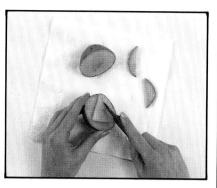

Paint some fabric paint on to the potato motif with a brush. Stamp off an excess paint on to some waste paper then print the motif on to your chosen fabric, leaving plenty of space for a second and even a third motif.

Cut another simple motif from the other half of the potato. Apply the colour as before and print on to the fabric. When the fabric has dried, iron on the back to fix the paints. Your fabric is now ready to be made up into cushions, curtains, blinds and so forth.

'QUILT' CUSHIONS

T hese cushions are based on designs taken from American patchwork quilts. With a soft pencil, copy the design on to tracing paper then position the trace, pencil marks down, over your chosen fabric. Transfer the image on to the fabric by tracing over the back of the design.

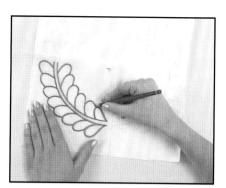

When the design is on the material, go over it with a pencil if the image is not strong enough. Apply the first colour using a fabric felt tip pen.

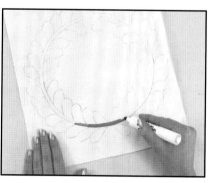

Fill in the other colours. If you are using alternate colours, as on these leaves, it is a good idea to mark each leaf with the correct colour so you don't make a mistake half way through. Iron on the back to fix the design and make the fabric up into cushions.

SALT ON SILK

Wonderful abstract patterns can be produced by sprinkling salt on freshly painted silk. Cut a piece of fine white silk lining and place in an embroidery frame, pulling taut. Select colours of silk paints you wish to use, shake and carefully open jars. Wet brush in water jar. Apply paint fairly swiftly and immediately sprinkle on salt. Fill frame with designs.

Leave to dry, then brush off salt. The silk will yield a variety of effects, so place different ready-cut window cards over the most attractive patterns. Mark area to be framed in window, then cut out slightly larger. The smaller the window, the more designs you can make. You could also add embroidery, beads and sequins to designs.

Mount silk in centre window of 3-fold card, using double-sided tape. Stick down left-hand portion of card over back of silk.

WHO'LL BE MY VALENTINE?

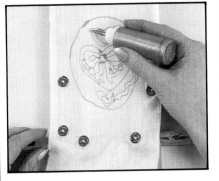 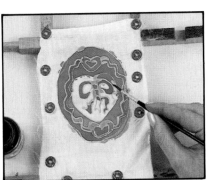

If you really love someone, you'll want to send him a beautiful Valentine's Day card, hand-crafted by you. To make it easier, you can buy the card blanks in most craft shops or haberdashery departments. The designs here are painted on silk. Stretch a piece of white silk over a frame (available from craft shops) and outline the design with gold gutta (see page 6).

Make sure the gutta lines are continuous so that the paint can't bleed through once the design is painted on. When the gutta is dry, apply the silk colours with a fine brush. Do not be over generous with the paint as the silk can only take so much before it is saturated and the colours start to bleed.

When the silk is dry, fix it according to the paint manufacturer's instructions. Then glue the silk in position on to the blank card and stick the mount down around it.

Home accessories provide a rich field for creative hands to get to work, both making new items and decorating existing ones. Using nothing more expensive than paper and cardboard you can make a lampshade, a handy letter rack and some novel pictures, or create original frames for existing photographs. Dingy old books can be rejuvenated by recovering them with hand-made marbled paper. Transform plain vases, lamp bases, candlesticks, plates and storage jars by painting them with simple or elaborate designs, or by applying the sponging and ragging techniques used on walls. Stencilling is another versatile art ideal for creating beautiful pictures and picture frames, or to bring an original touch to cheap white mugs and plates.

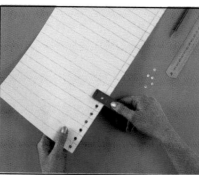

Co-ordinate your home with a pleated lampshade to match the wallpaper. For a 30cm (12in) wide shade cut a strip of wallpaper 130cm x 20cm (51in x 8in). On the wrong side, rule pleat lines across the strip 2cm (¾in) apart then draw a line along the length 1.2cm (½in) from the top. Punch a hole on this line between each pleat line.

Fold the strip in concertina pleats along the pleat lines. On the wrong side, slide each pleat into the punch in turn and make half a hole on the fold on the line. These holes will rest on the top section of the frame.

Overlap the ends of the lampshade and thread ribbon through the holes in the middle of each pleat. Draw up the pleats and slip the lampshade over the frame, resting the notches on top of the frame. Pull the ribbon ends to tighten the top and tie in a decorative bow.

Drop two or three colours onto the water and swirl together with the end of a paint brush. Cut plain paper to fit the tray. Wearing rubber gloves, start at one end of the tray and lower the paper onto the surface of the water so it can pick up the pattern. Carefully lift up the paper.

Leave the paper to dry overnight on newspaper. You can remove the paint from the tray by drawing strips of newspaper across the surface of the water.

The marbled paper can be used in many ways. Here, a plain book takes on a sophisticated look when recovered. Cut a rectangle of marbled paper large enough to wrap around the book with a 2.5cm (1in) margin on all sides. Wrap the paper around the book, open the cover and glue the paper inside the opening edges.

Prop up the book so the cover is open at a right angle. Snip the paper each side of the spine and stick the top and bottom margin inside the covers, folding under the corners.

Push the paper at the ends of the spine between the spine and the pages with the points of a pair of scissors. Arrange jewellery stones on the cover and use a strong glue to stick them in place. Cut two pieces of paper to fit inside the covers and glue inside.

There are many methods for marbling paper but this way needs little equipment. Fill a shallow tray with water. Put spots of enamel paint on the water with a paint brush. If they sink the paint is too thick and needs thinning with a little white spirit. If they disperse into a faint film it is too thin and should be mixed with more paint.

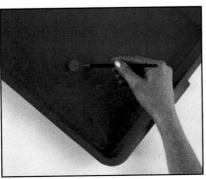

Stencil this attractive iris design on to thick watercolour paper for a linen texture and use wax stencil crayons for subtle colour shading. Size up the design on page 94 and cut three stencils for mauve, yellow and green areas. Tape the green stencil in place and blend together two green crayons. Rub the crayons on to the acetate and then collect the colour on to the brush.

Remove the green stencil and tape the mauve one in position, lining up the vertical and horizontal marks. Blend mauve, blue and turquoise for the flowers, shading the lower petals in mauve and the upper ones in blues, and getting deeper towards the centre of each flower. Lastly, use the yellow stencil. Work the brush in a light circular motion to shade the colours throughout.

Have an oval mount cut to fit around your stencil. Cut out the border stencil from the design on page 94 and try it out on scrap paper in various colours. Cut these trial pieces into strips and lay them around your mount. Hold them in place with masking tape and then insert a pin centrally at each corner when you are happy with the position.

Carefully remove the strips and, very lightly, mark guide lines for stencilling the border using a pencil and set-square. Check the lines are exactly the right distance from the oval shape and parallel to the outer edge. The stencils at the top and sides should be equidistant from the oval and the lower stencil slightly further away to look visually correct.

Finally, stencil the border in a single colour using stencil crayons as before. Build up the colour where the strips meet the round spots in the design to add interest. Assemble the stencil with the mount and a piece of glass in a simple frame coloured to complement your flowers and decorations.

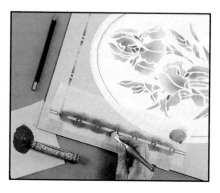

LETTER RACK

There is no excuse for mislaying letters with this smart letter rack. From thick mounting board cut a rectangle 24cm x 8cm (9½in x 3¼in) for the front and 24cm x 10cm (9½in x 4in) for the back. Diagonally trim away the top corners and cover one side of each piece with giftwrap.

Cut giftwrap slightly smaller than the front and back sections and glue in position on the wrong side. Take a piece of wood 24cm (9½in) long by 3cm (1¼in) wide and 1cm (⅜in) thick. Cover the wood with coloured paper.

Cut a rectangle of mounting board 27cm x 7cm (10½in x 2¾in) for the base and cover with coloured paper. Use a strong glue to stick the front to one narrow edge of the wood keeping the lower edges level. Glue the back to the other side in the same way. Finish the letter rack by gluing this upper section centrally to the base.

PRETTY AS A PICTURE

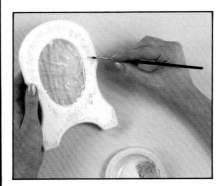

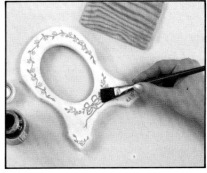

This pretty little frame is perfect for standing on a dressing table. Firstly, sand the frame until it is smooth and then give it a coat of white acrylic paint. Apply a second coat of paint if necessary and, when dry, draw the design with a soft pencil. Paint the design using acrylic paint in soft blues and greys with the flower centres in bright yellow.

Remove the backing and the glass and give the frame a protective coat of polyurethane varnish.

REGENCY SILHOUETTE

G ive your home a period touch with this classic decoration. You can use a clear profile sketch or a photograph as a basis for your picture. Make a tracing of the outline and place it face down on the back of a piece of black paper. Redraw the design to transfer it.

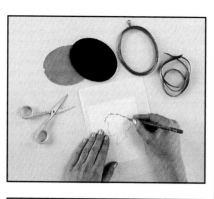

Cut out the motif with a pair of small, sharp scissors and glue the design to white paper. Trim the paper to fit your frame. Place the picture in the frame and glue a small ribbon bow to the top.

POT OF ANEMONES

T his delightful picture will brighten a dreary day. Cut a 3cm (1¼in) diameter circle of black paper; cut a fringe around the edge and a small hole in the centre. Cut a 6cm (2¼in) diameter circle of black tissue paper and wrap it over a small ball of cotton wool (absorbent cotton). Twist the edges together and insert into the hole.

Cut six petals from tissue paper and glue to the twisted end. Make two more flowers. Glue some striped wallpaper to a piece of cardboard and some cream paper over the lower third. From thick brown paper, cut a rectangle 13cm x 10cm (5in x 4in) for the pot and a strip 15cm x 2.5cm (6in x 1in) for the rim.

On one long edge of the pot mark 2.5cm (1in) from each end. Draw a line from the marks to the top corners and fold back the ends along the lines. Fold under 5mm (¼in) at the ends of the rim. Glue the folded ends of the pot to the background, slightly bowing the pot outwards. Glue the rim over the top in the same way. Glue flowers in place above the pot.

PHOTO FINISH

To make these smart frames, cut two pieces of mounting board 25cm x 19cm (10in x 7½in). Cut a window 17cm x 11cm (7in x 4½in) in the centre of one piece. Cut two pieces of giftwrap to cover the frames. Lay the window mount on the wrong side of one piece and cut a window in the giftwrap, leaving a 2cm (¾in) margin. Snip to the corners and glue the margins down.

Cover the back of the frame with giftwrap, then cut two 1cm (⅜in) wide strips of mounting board 18cm (7¼in) long and one 22cm (8½in) long. Cover with paper and glue to the wrong side of the back just inside three of the edges. Spread glue on the strips and carefully place the front of the frame on top, checking that the outer edges are level.

Cut a rectangle of mounting board 18cm x 6cm (7¼in x 2¼in) for the stand. Score across the stand 5cm (2in) from one end. Cover the stand with giftwrap and glue the scored end to the back with the other end level with either a long or short side depending on whether your photo is in landscape or portrait form. Bend the stand outwards.

BORDERLINES

The right mount can really enhance a picture. Buy a plain cardboard mount to fit your picture. Draw a 1cm (⅜in) wide border around the window with a pencil. Cut four 1cm (⅜in) wide strips of marbled paper. Spray the back of one strip with spray glue and place on the border. Cut off the ends diagonally at the corners with a craft knife.

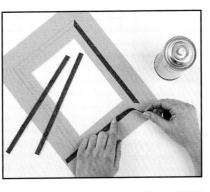

Apply the other strips to the mount, cutting the ends to meet diagonally in a mitred corner.

To complete the mount, draw a line each side of the border with a fine-tipped gold pen.

SPONGED VASE

An elegant but inexpensive vase is transformed with the simple use of a sponge and some ceramic paints. Take a small piece of natural sponge and dip it into some white spirit. Squeeze the sponge out and lightly dip it into a saucer of ceramic paint. Dab excess paint on to a piece of waste paper, then apply the colour to the vase with a light dabbing motion.

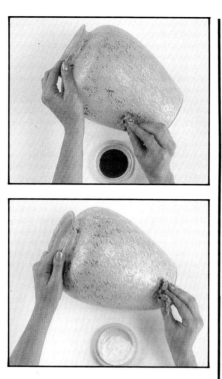

Sponge the whole of the vase, leaving space for a second colour, and re-applying paint to the sponge as necessary. Use a second sponge to apply the next colour, making sure to overlap the colours for an even finish. As an alternative to ceramic paints, you could use high gloss gold lacquer and ordinary emulsion paint.

RAG 'N' SPLASH

With a combination of ragging and flicking you can transform a plain china vase or jug into a work of art. You will need a piece of cloth for the ragging, a couple of fine artists' brushes and some ceramic paints. Dip the rag into one of the paints and then blot it onto some waste paper to remove any excess paint. Now begin to dab paint on to the vase.

Leave gaps between the dabs of paint to allow the background colour to show through. When you have evenly covered the surface, leave it to dry. Now spatter the vase with white ceramic paint, flicking the paint on with a fine brush. Once again, leave to dry.

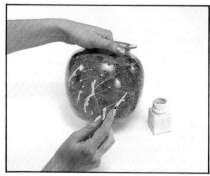

Finally, apply some gold ceramic paint with a fine paint brush, forming clusters of little gold dots across the surface of the vase. Be sure to clean your brush thoroughly in turpentine when you have finished.

DRAGONFLY LAMP

The inspiration for this lamp came from a small evening bag. Either copy the design used here or find an alternative source of inspiration, such as a piece of fabric, a greeting card or a porcelain plate. Then experiment with the colours you are going to use, colouring in the design with felt tip pens.

Trace your design on to the shade and colour it in using brightly coloured fabric felt tip pens. Edge the motifs in stronger colour. Now paint the design on to the lamp base using ceramic paints. If you do not feel confident about painting the shapes straight on to the surface, draw them on first with a chinagraph pencil.

Leave the first colour to dry before edging the design in a lighter shade. You will need to fix the paint on the lampshade by heating it with a hair dryer for a few minutes.

EMBROIDERED INSPIRATION

The inspiration for this vase comes from a beautiful piece of Victorian embroidery. The designs are similar except the white and black have been reversed so, instead of white stalks on a black background, there are black stalks on a white background. You can either copy this design, or find a similar piece of embroidery to copy.

As it is always difficult to paint directly on to a curved surface, first draw the design on to the vase using a chinagraph pencil.

Colour in the design with ceramic paints, mixing the various colours together to get the right shades. Use very fine paint brushes for the stalks and slightly thicker ones for the leaves and flowers. Clean the brushes carefully between each colour.

TULIP CANDLESTICKS

CRAZY CANDLES

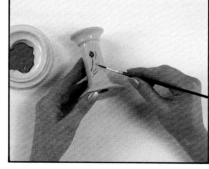

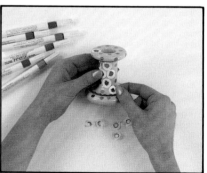

A simple motif such as a tulip can add style to the plainest of candlesticks. For this design you will need a pair of pink candlesticks, a fine paint brush and some garnet red and green ceramic paints. Decorate the top first, firmly holding the candlestick by the stem as you do so. Begin by painting the red flowers and clusters of tiny red dots, then fill in with green foliage.

Paint the stem and finally the base of the candlestick after the top has dried. Finish with lines of tiny red dots at the top and bottom of the stem, following the shape of the candlestick. Finally, when the paint is completely dry, apply a coat of ceramic varnish.

These candlesticks are designed for those in a party mood; they are bright and fun, and especially suitable for a teenage party. You will need some self-adhesive ring reinforcements, candlesticks, and multi-purpose felt tip paint pens in a range of bright colours. Stick the ring reinforcements all over the candlestick as shown.

Paint the centres of the circles in various colours. Once the paint is dry, pull off the reinforcements to reveal a series of coloured dots. Complete the design by painting a border line round the base of the stem in one of the bright colours you have been using. Finally, apply a coat of ceramic varnish.

FURTIVE FOOTPRINTS

W ho's been eating my porridge
. . . and left footprints all over
my plate? You can have great fun
decorating china like this, using bird
prints, paw prints, wellington boots or
even human footprints. To make the
paw print plate, first draw a spiral on
to the plate as shown with a
chinagraph pencil.

Using the spiral as a guide, paint the
outline of the prints in black ceramic
paint: you will need a very fine paint
brush for this. Once the paint has
dried, rub off all trace of the
chinagraph line.

Colour the centre of the paws with a
brightly coloured ceramic paint. When
the plate is completely dry, finish off
with a protective coat of ceramic
varnish.

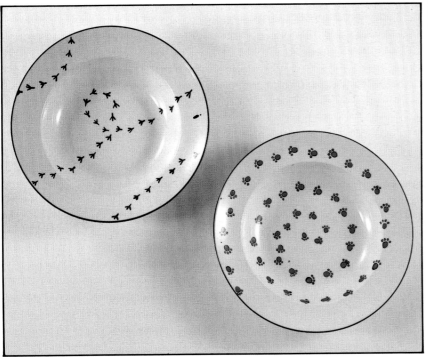

HARVEST STORAGE JARS

B ring the countryside into your
kitchen with these charming
storage jars. Cut out a piece of paper
to fit round the side of the jar and
then, using the template on page 95,
draw your design on to the paper. To
work out your colour scheme, colour
the design using felt tip pens. Trace off
the design on to the jar and outline the
pencil with a fine black felt tip pen.

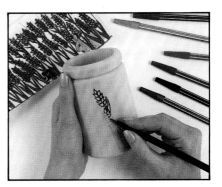

Colour the corn with the coloured felt
tip pens, leaving the middle of some of
the husks the natural wood colour so
that the corn looks more rounded and
realistic. Paint the centre of some of
the other husks yellow to add more
interest. Do not press the pens too
hard as the colour will bleed.

Colour in the animals and butterflies
and decorate around the top edge of
the jar with green, as shown in the
main picture, to suggest hills. Paint
the lid with swallows soaring in the
sunshine and, when the inks are dry,
finish with a coat of polyurethane
varnish to protect the colour.

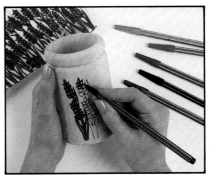

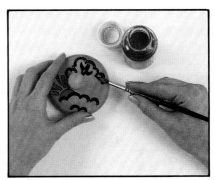

ZIG-ZAG TUMBLERS

These octagonal glasses look very stylish with a band of colour rotating around the glass. You will need either ceramic or glass paint. Cut four or five strips of masking tape long enough to wind from the top of the glass down to the bottom. Stick the first strip down then add successive strips, leaving a gap between each one.

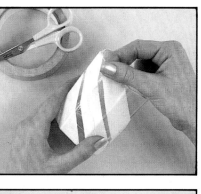

Apply the paint to the exposed areas, holding on to the masking tape while you rotate the glass. Now leave the glass to dry.

Remove the masking tape. If some of the paint has seeped under the tape, clean it off with a cloth dipped in turpentine.

TORN TAPE PLATE

Create a stunning design on ceramics by masking off areas with torn tape. Cut a strip of masking tape the width of your plate and very carefully rip it in half lengthways, creating an uneven edge. Place the two torn pieces back to back across the centre of the plate. Then add further double strips of tape either side, leaving gaps in between each set.

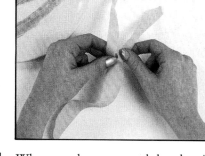

When you have covered the plate in torn tape lines, make sure that all the edges are stuck down properly. Apply ceramic paint to the exposed areas, using a dabbing motion so that the paint does not seep under the tape.

Leave the plate to dry for at least 24 hours before carefully removing the tape. Clean up any smudged edges using a rag dipped in white spirit, then apply a coat of ceramic varnish. The black lines on a white background gives a striking 'zebra stripe' effect, but other colour combinations look equally attractive, so try experimenting a little.

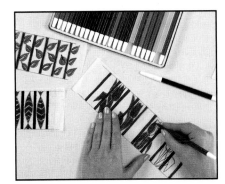

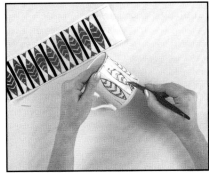

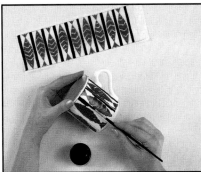

These mugs have been stencilled using low tack masking peel. Choose mugs with straight sides, and not ones which curve out at the top, so that the masking peel will stick properly. Cut out a piece of paper to fit exactly round the mug and, following the templates on page 95, draw the design. Work out your colour scheme using felt tip pens that match the colours of the paints.

Place the low tack peel on top of the design and trace the design on to the peel using an indelible pen. Pull off the backing paper and stick the masking film on to the mug. Then cut out the design with a stencil or craft knife.

Using ceramic paint and a fine brush, apply the first colour. Try to hold the brush as upright as possible so that you don't get too much seepage under the stencil.

When the paint is dry apply the next colour and so on until the design is complete. Leave to dry, then peel off the masking film. Clean up any rough edges with a stencil knife or a fine brush soaked in turpentine. Finally, apply a coat of ceramic varnish to protect the design.

TABLECLOTHS AND NAPKINS

In this section, you will find many different ways to give your tablecloths and napkins an individual touch. The designs on the following pages show how a combination of napkin and tablecloth works together to accentuate an overall theme. There are attractive alternatives to the traditional damask cloth using such materials as paints, ribbons and flowers. Napkins are also a necessary element of all table settings, however informal, and a variety of folds as well as craft ideas will enhance your setting. The most important requirement for folding napkins is that the napkin should be well starched and pressed.

Although designed for a Thanksgiving or Harvest Festival dinner, this setting could be used at any time of the year. The 'placemat' is really an outline printed on a plain white cloth, using a potato cut in a leaf shape; the napkin uses the same motif. Wooden-handled cutlery, hand-blown glass and dried flowers help to set the rustic theme.

ABSTRACT TABLECLOTH

Transform a plain tablecloth with this eyecatching design. Choose a brush the correct size for your design, and use a paint suitable for fabrics. (Because the paint is applied quite thickly, a paper tablecloth is not suitable.)

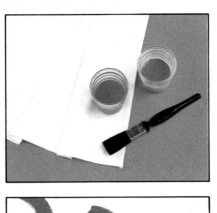

Practice first on a spare piece of cloth or paper, dipping the brush into the paint for each new stroke. Then paint the cloth, applying the lighter colour first; allow it to dry thoroughly.

Paint on the second colour in broad sweeps, allowing the paint to fade off towards the end of each brushstroke. Follow the manufacturer's instructions for fixing the fabric paint.

POTATO PRINT 'PLACEMAT'

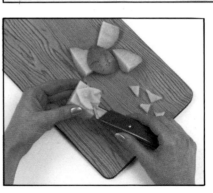

Why not decorate a plain white tablecloth with a placemat outline to match your china? All you need is a raw potato and some paint. First cut the potato into a cube about the size of your chosen motif. The leaf shape shown here is about 3cm (1¼in) square. Using a sharp knife, cut the motif on one side of the cube as shown.

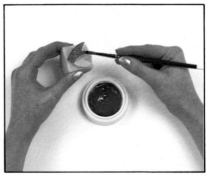

Use a paint suitable for fabric, or a water-based paint if you are printing on a paper tablecloth. Spread the paint evenly over the raised motif.

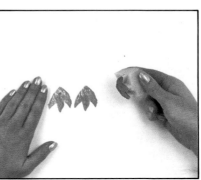

On a piece of stiff paper, draw the outline of the 'placemat' in black felt-tip pen. Place this under the cloth as a guide when printing. Press the potato down onto the cloth, taking care not to smudge it. Practice first on a spare piece of paper. The same technique can be used to print a border design around the edge of the napkin.

RAG-ROLLED TABLECLOTH

FLOWER-STREWN TABLECLOTH

This simple idea can transform an ordinary tablecloth into something special. Choose a plain white or pastel-coloured tablecloth and artificial flowers with small blossoms. You will also need some green sewing thread and a needle.

Rag-rolling, or ragging, is a quick and easy way to transform a plain fabric or paper tablecloth. Pour a water-based paint or fabric dye onto a plate, and dip a crumpled piece of cloth in it. Blot the cloth on some waste paper or fabric to remove excess paint.

If the flowers you have chosen have several blooms to a stem, trim them into individual sprigs. Set aside the remaining leaves.

Lightly press the crumpled fabric onto a spare piece of paper or cloth to practice getting an even amount of paint over the area to be covered. Once you feel confident, rag the tablecloth, adding a second colour (once the first has dried) if desired. If using fabric dye, follow the manufacturer's instructions for fixing the colour.

Sew the flower sprigs to the cloth. You can use as many or as few sprigs as you wish; you could sew one or two by each place setting or, for a stunning effect, cover the whole cloth with them — leaving room for place settings and serving dishes. Place the leftover leaves with a single flower sprig on each guest's plate.

FLEUR-DE-LYS TABLECLOTH

RIBBON-TRIMMED TABLECLOTH

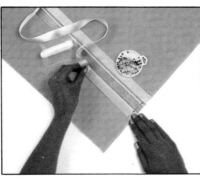

A dd a touch of luxury to a dinner party by decorating your own tablecloth in gold. First choose a simple image, such as the fleur-de-lys motif shown here. You can either decorate an existing cloth or buy a length of wide inexpensive cotton fabric. Draw the shape in pencil first, and then go over it in gold paint.

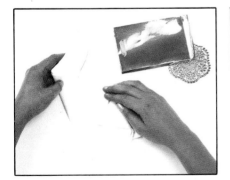

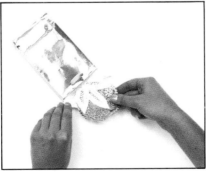

To echo the shape of the fleur-de-lys symbol you can dress up your table napkins as shown. A napkin with a lacy edge will look best. Fold the napkin into a square. Keeping the lacy edge nearest to you, fold the left- and right-hand corners in to overlap one another. Fold the remaining point in to meet them.

Slide the napkin, lacy edge towards you, into a shining foil gift bag. Because both napkin and china are white, a lacy gold coaster was inserted into the bag, underneath the lace detail on the napkin to give it more definition.

T his pretty tablecloth isn't hard to make but requires a bit of patience. You can make the cloth yourself or buy one ready-made. Buy enough ribbon in each colour to run along four sides of the cloth, plus 24cm (8in) if using a ready-made cloth. Position the ribbons as shown, with fusible webbing underneath (omitting the area where they will cross), and pin them in place.

Continue to pin the ribbons in place along all the edges, making sure that you keep them straight. Thread the ribbons underneath one another to create a lattice effect, as shown. If you are using a ready-made cloth, allow the ribbons to overlap the edge by 3cm (1in); this will be folded under later.

Replace the corner pins with tacking (basting) stitches, if you are working on an un-hemmed cloth; this provides extra stability. Press the ribbons in place with a warm iron, removing pins as you go and stopping just short of the tacking. Finally, hem the edges. On a ready-made cloth, sew the ribbon ends to the wrong side by hand.

THE BUTTERFLY

THE PRINCESS

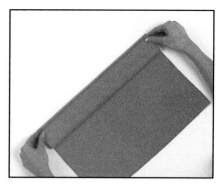

Fold the napkin in half to form a crease along the centre line. Then open the napkin out again. Fold one half of the napkin lengthwise into three by bringing the top edge of the square inwards to the centre line and then folding it back on itself as shown. Repeat with the second half.

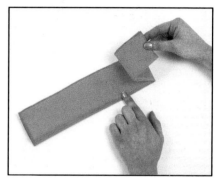

Fold the napkin in half lengthwise by tucking one half under the other along the centre line. Lay the resulting strip flat with the three folded edges facing you. Mark the centre of this strip with a finger and fold the right-hand edge in towards the centre and back on itself as shown. Repeat with the left-hand side.

A crisply starched napkin is required for this pretty fold. Lay the napkin flat. Fold two edges to meet in the centre as shown. Then fold the half nearest you across the centre line and over on the top of the other half, to form a long, thin rectangle.

Pull the top left-hand corner across towards the top right-hand corner to create a triangle, pressing down gently along the folds to hold them in place. Repeat with the remaining left-hand folds, and then do the same with all the right-hand folds. Ease the folds open slightly and display the napkin with the centre point facing the guest.

Fold the right-hand end of the rectangle in towards the centre, and with another fold double it back on itself as shown. Repeat with the left-hand side so that the double folds meet in the centre.

Pull the right-hand back corner across to the left, bringing the front edge across the centre line to form a triangle. Anchoring the right hand side of the triangle with one hand, use the other hand to fold the corner back to its original position, thus creating the 'wings' of the arrangement. Repeat the process on the left-hand side.

PURE AND SIMPLE

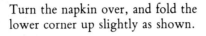

This elegant napkin fold is easier to produce than it looks. First fold the napkin in half diagonally, then bring the left- and right-hand corners up to meet at the apex.

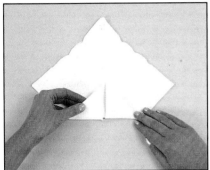

Turn the napkin over, and fold the lower corner up slightly as shown.

Fold the left- and right-hand corners underneath the napkin on a slight diagonal, pressing the folds lightly in place.

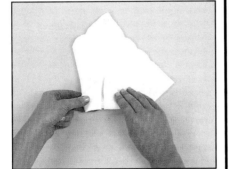

THE BISHOP'S HAT

This mitre-shaped fold can be displayed either on a flat surface (as above) or in a glass, cup or soup bowl, which allows the flaps to drape gracefully over the sides. Begin by folding the napkin diagonally to form a triangle, then pull each corner up to the apex as shown to form a square.

Turn the napkin over so that the free edges lie towards you. Pull the two top flaps up and away from you; then fold the remaining two flaps back in the same way to form a triangle.

Carefully turn the napkin over once more, and pull the two outer corners together so that they overlap; tuck one flap into the folds of the other to hold them in place. Finally, turn the front of the 'hat' to face you, position the napkin upright and pull the loose flaps down as shown in the main picture.

DOUBLE JABOT

ORIENTAL FAN

Fold the napkin twice to form a square and position it with the loose corners at the top right. Fold the top corner back diagonally to meet the lower left corner, then turn it back on itself as shown. Continue to fold the corner back and forth to create a 'concertina' effect along the diagonal strip of napkin.

Lift the next layer of fabric from the top right-hand corner and repeat the process described above to create two parallel strips with zigzag edges.

This highly effective design benefits from a well-starched napkin and is very easy to make. Begin by folding the napkin in half lengthwise and then fold one end of the oblong backwards and forwards in concertina- or accordion-style folds, until just past the halfway point.

Holding the folds firmly together, fold the napkin lengthwise down the middle to bring both ends of the 'concertina' together. Keeping the folds in position in one hand, fold the loose flap of the napkin over across the diagonal.

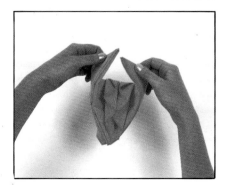

Pick the napkin up in both hands with the zigzag folds in the centre. Fold it in half diagonally to form a triangle, keeping the pleats on the outside. Take the right-hand and left-hand corners of the triangle and curl them back, tucking one into the other to secure them. Stand the napkin upright on a plate as shown.

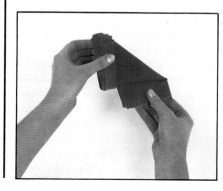

Push the flap underneath the support as shown to balance the napkin, and, letting go of the pleats, allow the fan to fall into position.

PURE ELEGANCE

For best results use a crisply starched napkin to make this attractive fold. First fold the napkin lengthwise into three to form a long rectangle. Lay it horizontally with the free edge away from you, and fold the left- and right-hand ends in to meet in the centre.

Fold down the top right- and left-hand corners to meet in the centre, forming a point. Take the napkin in both hands and flip it over towards you so that the point is facing you and the flat side of the napkin is uppermost.

Lift the sides and pull them over towards one another to form a cone shape. Tuck the left-hand corner into the right-hand corner to secure it. Turn the napkin around and place it on a plate as shown in the main picture.

DOUBLE CORNET

This design looks best in a conical glass but can be adapted for a wider-based container. Although it takes a little more practice than most, it is worth the effort. First lay the napkin flat and fold it in three lengthwise. Position it as shown, with the free edge on top.

Take hold of the top left-hand and right-hand corners of the napkin with the index finger and thumb of each hand. Roll the corners diagonally towards you as shown.

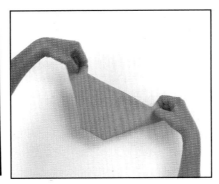

Without releasing your hold on the napkin, continue to roll the corners inwards in one sweeping movement by swivelling both hands and napkin down, up and over until your hands are together palms uppermost. By now the napkin should be rolled into two adjacent flutes. Release your hands and place the napkin in a glass, arranging it neatly.

LACY NAPKIN BOW

THANKSGIVING NAPKIN

This simple place setting is perfect for a Thanksgiving or Harvest Festival dinner. Use a sisal or straw placemat and a plain white napkin. For the decoration you will need a selection of dried flowers and grasses and three lengths of beige or wheat-coloured ribbon, each about 50cm (20in) long.

Tie the lengths of ribbon together at one end. Plait them until the plait is long enough to tie around the napkin twice with a little left over.

Ideal for a wedding or anniversary dinner, this lacy napkin bow is not only pretty but also easy to make. The napkins themselves should be pretty, preferably with a lace detail around the edge. For each napkin you will need about 90cm (1yd) of wide satin ribbon and the same amount of insertion lace.

Group the bunch of dried flowers and grasses together, securing them with thread or twine. Fold the napkin in half twice to form a long, thin rectangle. Lay the flowers on top of the napkin. Wind the plaited ribbon around the napkin and flowers twice and tie the ends under the napkin.

For best results, the napkin should be starched and well ironed and folded into quarters. To cut decorative points for the ribbons and lace, fold the ends as shown and cut them diagonally.

Fold under two corners of the napkin to overlap in the centre, forming the shape shown here. Iron the folds flat. Lay the ribbon and lace flat, wrong side up, with the ribbon on top. Place the napkin on top and tie the ribbon and lace around it in a bow.

FLORAL NAPKIN RING

This charming flower-trimmed napkin ring adds a touch of elegance to a table setting and is very easy to make. Bend a short length of florists' wire into a circle; twist the ends together to secure them.

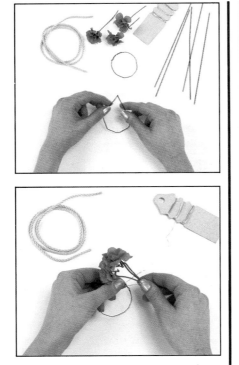

Wind some fine fuse wire around one or two small silk flowers — chosen to co-ordinate with your china and table linen. Then twist the ends of the fuse wire around the circle of florist's wire to hold the flowers in place.

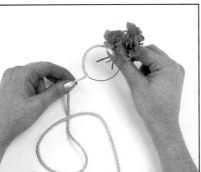

For covering the ring choose a fine ribbon or decorative braid. Hold one end in place with one hand, and use the other hand to twist the braid around the circle to cover it completely, beginning and ending underneath the flowers. Secure the ends with glue. Insert the napkin and add a fresh flower for the finishing touch.

DECORATED NAPKINS

Here are a couple of ideas for jazzing up ordinary paper napkins. For the blue napkin, cut a star shape from a piece of cardboard — the cardboard must be slightly wider than the folded napkin. Hold the cardboard firmly in place over the napkin and spray silver or gold paint over the area. Let the paint dry for several minutes before you allow anything else to touch it.

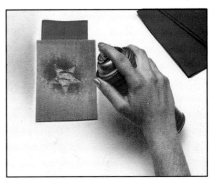

The white napkins have a design stencilled on them with oil-based stencil crayons. You can buy these separately or in packs, with ready-cut stencils. Choose your design, then place it over the area you want to stencil — in this case the corner of the napkin. Rub the crayon over a spare area of stencil, then take the colour up onto the brush and paint it over the stencil, in a circular motion.

Use the brush only over the parts you wish to show up in that colour. Now switch to the next colour. It is best to use a different brush for each colour if you want clear colour definition.

Place cards have traditionally been used to organize the seating at large banquets. But instead of only thinking of them as formal and ceremonious, we should see them as adding an element of fun and individuality to a table. The novel designs on the following pages range from comic and colourful to pretty and elegant, so they can be used in either formal or casual settings.

Placemats are simple to make and they can be matched to any party theme. They are the perfect alternative to a tablecloth, and those that are easy to clean are particularly suitable for children's parties.

A harlequin theme prevails in this striking table setting — perfect for a fancy-dress party. The chequered square place card sits in a black-stemmed cocktail glass, with a pink streamer tumbling gracefully over the edge. You can also make cardboard or papier màché harlequin masks for each guest; or you can just make two and place them back to back to form a centrepiece.

HARLEQUIN PLACE CARD

M̲ake cocktail glasses look extra smart with this chequered place card. First cut a 7.5cm (3in) square from a piece of stiff white cardboard. Use a pencil and ruler to mark off 2.5cm (1in) divisions and join these up to form a grid. Colour in alternate squares with a black felt pen to give a chequer-board pattern.

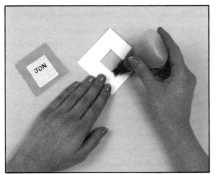

On a 5cm (2in) square of cardboard write the name. Cut out a 6cm-(2½in)-square piece of pink net fabric; set it aside. Using a sharp craft knife, cut out the centre of the chequered card to leave a hole 2.5cm (1in) square. Turn the card over and apply some glue around the edges of the hole.

Place the piece of net over the card with the name, and hold them together in one hand while positioning the chequered card diagonally over the top. Press firmly to apply the glue to all three surfaces. Leave the card to dry for a few minutes.

HARLEQUIN PLACEMAT

T̲his unusual placemat is easily made from cardboard and a wallpaper border. A black and white border has been chosen to co-ordinate with the table setting. Cut a 30cm (12in) square from a sheet of thick cardboard, using a steel rule and craft knife to ensure precision.

Cut the border into four strips, allowing a little extra on each strip for trimming. Apply double-sided tape to the back of each strip, but do not peel off the protective backing yet. Lay two adjacent strips in place; where they meet at the corners, try to match the pattern repeat. Holding one strip on top of the other, cut diagonally across the corner.

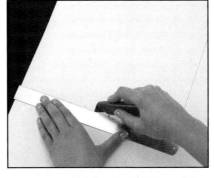

Holding each strip in place along its inner edge, begin to peel back the protective paper from the double-sided tape, as shown. Rub a soft cloth along the border as you peel to stick it in place.

COLOURFUL CUPCAKES

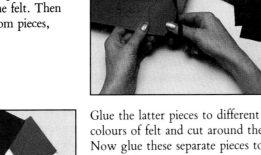

To break the ice at a kids' party make these delightful iced cupcake name badges. Trace the shape from one of those shown in the main picture. Cut each cake shape from thin cardboard as a base for the felt. Then cut out the top and bottom pieces, again in cardboard.

Glue the latter pieces to different colours of felt and cut around them. Now glue these separate pieces to the base card.

Finish off by sticking a name label to the front of the bun and a little double-sided tape to the back. When the little guests arrive simply tear off the backing from the tape and label them!

COLLAGE PLACE CARD

This collage place card can be made from wrapping paper and scraps of plain stiff paper. Select a gift-wrapping paper with a design that is appropriate to the theme of your party and plain paper in a harmonizing colour. Cut a rectangle of the plain paper about 14 by 9cm (5½ by 3½in) and fold it in half as shown.

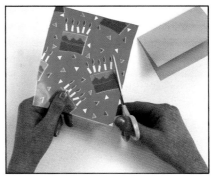

Cut around the shape you have decided to use and stick this to the card with double-sided tape or glue.

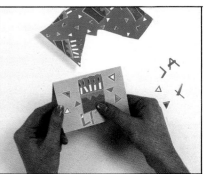

Stick additional shapes onto the card as desired. Put double-sided tape onto the back of a small area of the wrapping paper, and cut thin strips with which to make up the names. Peel off the backing and attach the strips to the card to form the letters.

RICEPAPER FANS PLACE CARD

Tiny pleated fans decorate these pastel place cards. From pale pastel stiff paper cut a rectangle about 9 by 12cm (3½ by 5in). From darker paper cut a rectangle about 5mm (¼in) shorter and narrower. Cut several thin strips from a sheet of ricepaper, and fold them concertina-style as shown.

Allowing 10 or 12 folds per fan, snip the folded strips into several pieces. Pinch them at one end to form tiny fans. Fold the two rectangles in half, and place the darker one over the other. Lightly glue them in place. Cut a small rectangle from the paler paper for the name; glue it onto the front of the card.

Put several dabs of glue on the card and glue the fans in place as shown.

FLORAL PLACE CARD

This charming place card looks especially good on floral china. Cut the posies from Victorian floral transfers, or from magazines, seed catalogues or greeting cards.

Cut a piece of thin white cardboard about 10 by 8cm (4 by 3in). Group the flower shapes on the card as shown. Once you have created a pleasing arrangement, glue the shapes in place on the card. Set it aside to dry.

Cut a strip of pastel-coloured stiff paper, and write the name on it. Set it aside. Cut around the flower shapes, leaving a 1cm (½in) strip of white cardboard along the bottom. Fold this backwards to form a stand for the place card. A tiny posy of dried lavender can be placed on each plate alongside the card.

TARTAN PLACE CARD

For a traditional Hogmanay or Burns Night celebration, make tartan place cards for your guests. Use plaid ribbon and either white or coloured lightweight cardboard, and add a kilt pin for the finishing touch.

Cut a rectangle of cardboard about 10 by 12cm (4 by 5in), or a size to fit the plate. Fold it in half, and write the name on the left-hand side. Cut a piece of ribbon to edge the card front and back, allowing a little extra to turn under the edges.

Stick ribbon onto the card with fabric glue, folding the excess underneath as shown. Pin the kilt pin through the ribbon and card to complete the authentically Scottish look.

VALENTINE PLACE CARD

Heart-shaped place cards are perfect for a romantic dinner or Valentine's Day supper. Using the template provided, trace heart shapes onto shiny red and plain white lightweight cardboard, and carefully cut them out.

Write the person's name on the white heart. Punch or cut a hole at the top of each heart, and thread a thin red ribbon through the hole. To add the finishing touches, tie the cutlery together with a wider ribbon, making a pretty bow. Then loosely tie the place cards to the bow, securing the cutlery as shown above.

KITE PLACE CARDS

These colourful place cards are perfect for a children's party. For each kite you will need stiff paper in two colours. From each colour cut two rectangles, each 10 by 15cm (4 by 6in). Draw a line down the centre, then another line at right angles across it, 5cm (2in) from one end. Join up the points, then cut off the four corners; set them aside.

Use two of the corners of the red card to decorate the yellow kite, glueing them in place as shown. Similarly, use two of the leftover pieces of the yellow card to decorate the red kite. Write the name on each kite.

Cut out squares of coloured tissue, allowing three for each kite. On the back of each kite, glue a 40cm (16in) strip of thin ribbon. Pinch the squares of tissue together in the centre and tie the ribbon around them. Cut a small strip of cardboard, fold it in two and glue it to the back of the kite; use this hook to attach the kite to a glass.

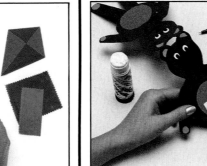

TEDDY BEARS' PICNIC

Teddy not only tells the little ones where to sit, but can be taken home afterwards as a little party gift. Draw a teddy shape using your favourite bear as inspiration and folding the paper at the top to produce a double shape as shown. Cut the shape from a spongy textured paper or from felt. Now glue this to some brown cardboard and carefully cut around it.

Now cut out two yellow circular tummies, some pink ears and paws — the forepaws slightly smaller than the back ones — black and white eyes and black noses, all from felt. The mouth is a tiny piece of black yarn. Glue all these in place.

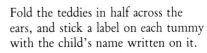

Fold the teddies in half across the ears, and stick a label on each tummy with the child's name written on it.

FLOWER DECORATIONS

The beauty of the fresh flower arrangements shown in this chapter, whether stood in vases or floated in water, is necessarily short-lived. But once you get into the art of using dried flowers (see page 9) many more-permanent home decorations become possible. You can use the dried blooms to decorate boxes, or to create table centres, wreaths and pomanders which would be costly to buy. Add essential oils and create rose-scented pot pourri, or decorate a straw hat with a mixture of dried flowers, silk flowers and ribbons. The dried flowers available will vary according to your sources of supply, but you should be able to get all the most popular ones, such as achillea, lavender, rosebuds, helichrysum (straw flower), larkspur, sunray, statice (sea lavender), amaranthus and gypsophila. Many dried flowers are small and unimpressive individually, but once grouped together with others they create a uniquely beautiful effect. Dried grasses such as the fluffy rabbit's or hare's tail grass, can provide dramatic contrast, as do seed heads like poppy, physalis and honesty.

For a summer table centrepiece nothing can surpass the beauty of flowers. The tall jug contains a mixture of anemones, ranunculus, kaffir lily (*Schizostylis*) and white September flowers (aster), the mixture of shapes providing variety. The smallest vase contains a tiny narcissus, ranunculus and anemones with a few heads of love-in-a-mist (*Nigella*).

This fat, rounded jug has a fairly wide neck and is therefore ideal for full-blown roses, which look good clustered together to form a close, rounded shape. Delicate stalks of white September flowers (aster) and a few heads of love-in-a-mist (*Nigella*) show up well against the pale pink roses and give more definition to the arrangement.

ALIGHT WITH FLOWERS

Flowers are definite favourites when it comes to centrepieces, so here's an attractive variation on a theme. Use a wide-necked bowl, either glass or ceramic, and fill it with water to about 2cm (1in) below the rim. Then, snipping their stalks off close to the head, arrange some flowers on the surface of the water.

Flowers with large heads, such as the tulips and roses used here, are the easiest kind to float. But a few small orchids, with their interesting outline, add contrast to the arrangement.

Finally, add three or four floating candles. (Be careful not to overload the bowl with flowers, for they could catch fire once the candles are lit!)

FLOATING ANEMONES

This arrangement makes an ideal centrepiece for any table but especially a low coffee table where the pretty faces of the anemones can be seen to their best advantage. Half fill a clear glass bowl with water. Then select 12 to 15 anemones and cut their stems down to around 2-3cm (1-1½in).

Place the anemone heads on the surface of the water and intersperse with little clumps of *Viburnum tinus* to add contrast.

A second smaller bowl looks very attractive with the main arrangement and helps to break up the symmetry of the outline. Fill a smaller bowl with large shining marbles and water. Then position just two or three anemone heads on the surface with a little sprig of gypsophilia (also known as baby's breath in the United States) so that the marbles can still be seen.

DECORATED BOX

C hoose an attractive box. If it needs recovering this can be done using lining paper and then painting it, or using wrapping paper or wallpaper. Fabric is another possibility, but if you are adding flowers try to keep the fabric as plain as possible. Make wired loops of lace or ribbon and glue them onto the lid of the box with a hot glue gun.

Depending on the size of the box, choose fairly large or special flowers rather than a mass of smaller flowers. The box illustrated is decorated with peonies, which make a wonderful focal point.

Finish the lid with smaller dried flowers to blend with the lace or ribbon and peonies and soften the arrangement.

LAVENDER AND ROSE BASKET

C hoose a basket, then glue a green plastic frog, which holds dried flower foam in place, into the base of the basket. Place a trimmed block of dried flower foam in the basket, impaled on the prongs of the frog. Cover the foam with sea lavender as a base for the other flowers. Then add several bunches of dried lavender: this adds a delightful colour as well as perfume.

Add dried roses of your choice. The ones shown here are a champagne colour and very pretty, but you could also use pink or peach. Roses are well worth drying yourself as they are expensive to buy.

Make double loops with some pretty ribbon and wire the base of each loop. Secure these loops either side of the handles, as a finishing touch.

FLORAL PHOTO FRAME

Make a small bundle of lavender by wiring a few fresh or dried stems together, and attach a narrow satin ribbon bow.

Using a hot glue gun, attach the lavender bundle and bow to a photograph frame.

As a finishing touch, add some dried pink rosebuds, using the hot glue gun.

ROSEBUD POMANDER

This little rosebud ball is simply lovely. The rosebuds can be obtained from a specialist dried flower supplier or from a shop that sells loose pot pourri. You will need 3 or 4 handfuls of rosebuds, a 7.5 cm (3 in) dried flower foam ball, three 15 cm (6 in) lengths of medium gauge florist's wire, 30-35 cm (12-14 in) lengths of ribbon and one of lace.

Make a loop with the length of lace and wrap a wire around the ends, leaving a leg that is at least 10 cm (4 in) long. Push this wire straight through the foam ball and out the other side. Bend the end over to make a hook and push it back up into the foam to secure it in place. The ribbons can then be wired in the same way, but with shorter legs, and just pushed into the ball.

Take a rosebud and, starting near the point where the ribbon meets the foam ball, press the short stem into the foam. Continue to press in rosebuds, either in a random pattern or in straight lines, until the ball is completely covered. Take care to sort out the rosebuds first, so you use only the best shapes, sizes and colours.

GERANIUM POT POURRI

This subtle and aromatic pot pourri is especially suitable for a kitchen or dining room. You will need a handful of each of the following dried ingredients: scented geranium leaves, marjoram and oregano flowers, mint leaves and flowers, and blue cornflowers. You will also need 15 ml (1 tbsp) orris root powder and 15 drops rose geranium essential oil.

Remove the stalks from all the flowers and leaves, then gently mix together the ingredients in a bowl. Add the orris root powder and mix again. Finally, add the drops of rose geranium essential oil and mix well until all the oil has been absorbed. Put the mixture into a polythene bag and seal well. Leave for 2 weeks, shaking occasionally.

When the pot pourri has matured, shake well before turning it out of the bag into the container of your choice. Place some of the large, more interesting pieces on top of the bowl as a decoration.

ROSE POT POURRI

A gorgeous, traditional fragrance to perfume any room in the house, this pot pourri also makes a stunning decoration. You will need 15 ml (1 tbsp) each of dried red rose petals, lavender, pink rosebuds and dried orange peel, 4 or 5 broken cinnamon sticks, 5 ml (1 tsp) orris root powder, 15 drops rose essential oil and some dried whole roses for decoration.

Place all the ingredients, except the oil and whole roses, in a bowl and mix with a metal spoon. Do not use a plastic or wooden spoon as it will absorb the oil. Add the 15 drops of essential oil and gently mix again until all the oil is absorbed into the mixture. Put the pot pourri into a polythene bag and seal tightly, then leave to mature for 2 weeks, shaking occasionally.

Empty the mixture into the bowl that you want to use for the display, then decorate the top with some whole roses that have been air dried or, better still, dried in silica gel crystals. The mixture can be revived when necessary by adding more oil and stirring well.

COUNTRY-STYLE STRAW HAT

This wonderful hat is very easy to make at home, especially if you have a hot glue gun: other types of glue are much weaker and more difficult to use. As well as the hat, you will need a bow, some large silk flowers and leaves and some smaller varieties of silk flowers. This design features silk peonies, larkspur and gypsophila, plus some dried sea lavender.

Glue the ribbon bow on to the centre back of the hat and then attach some sea lavender with the hot glue gun. If you wish to use only silk flowers, as opposed to a mixture of silk and dried ingredients, substitute something similar that would make a good base and fill out the design – some pieces of silk hydrangea heads or a larger quantity of the gypsophila are ideal.

When you are happy with the shape of the basic ingredients around the hat, glue on the largest flowers and some leaves. You can either place these in random groups or symmetrically around the brim. Any full, many-petalled flowers are suitable, such as roses, carnations, gardenias or camellias.

Finally, glue on the smaller, more delicate items, which in this case are larkspur and gypsophila. These finer ingredients fill the brim and add a dainty look which balances well with the larger, more dominant flowers. As a final touch you could scent the hat by dropping some essential oil onto the flowers.

Next, make a ring of wire mesh, slightly deeper than the container and wide enough to fit snuggly round it. The ring must be double thickness so you can pack it with dry sphagnum moss. When it is fully packed, neatly bend the raw edges of wire over to close the ring. Now cut several equal lengths of birch twigs and attach them to the moss ring using wire pins — two per twig.

Cover the wire pins by tying long strands of raffia around the ring. Once the plaster has set, place the container inside the wire surround. Take a large sphere of florists' foam and scrape out the centre using a knife. Press the ball on to the wooden 'stem' of the tree, making sure it is held firm. Now wire some small bunches of flowers, leaving at least 3cm (1in) of wire 'tail'.

The flowers used here are orange and yellow helichrysum (strawflower or everlasting), blue larkspur and green amaranthus (love-lies-bleeding). Use the helichrysum first to form the shape, keeping the arrangement spherical. Next add the larkspur and amaranthus, making sure they do not protrude too far out of the arrangement and break up the shape.

This ever-popular form of floral arrangement is not as difficult to achieve as you might think. Begin by selecting a suitable container for the base. Mix up some plaster of Paris with water and fill the container. Quickly insert an interestingly-shaped branch for the stem, holding it in position for a couple of minutes until the plaster begins to set.

Finish off by putting pieces of moss around the base of the tree to hide the plaster of Paris and the wire mesh.

This beautiful design makes the perfect decoration for Valentine's day. Take some dry, bendy silver birch twigs, trim off all the rough ends and divide them into two equal bundles, about 60cm (24in) long. Join the two bundles at one end with stub wires; and again about 20cm (8in) further along. Now bend either side round to form a heart shape as shown.

Bind the three ends firmly with wire, then wrap wire around four other points on the heart to hold the twigs together. Cover each of the wired areas with red satin or gift wrap ribbon, gluing each strip in place at the back. Wire up a couple of red bows (as described on page 9) and put one on either side of the heart.

Attach a length of wired ribbon to the top of the heart for hanging. To soften the effect, take small clumps of gypsophila (baby's breath) and push them in between the ribbon bands and the twigs. To finish off, mix some more gypsophila with some tiny red spray roses and position them at the base of the heart.

Bring a touch of the country into your living room with this beautiful array of garden flowers. Take a wicker shopping basket and fill the top with wire mesh, attaching the mesh to the sides of the basket with wire. Form a base for the arrangement by packing the mesh with wired bunches of sea lavender.

Wire clumps of love-in-a-mist and insert them into the arrangement so that they stand out above the sea lavender. Then start to fill in with bunches of soft pink larkspur. Try to keep the arrangement slightly parted around the handle so that the latter is not totally obscured. Finish filling in with bunches of lady's mantle, then add several garden roses to complete the picture.

PRETTY POSIES

This little collection of hanging baskets would be a pretty addition to a bedroom or bathroom. Take three small straw baskets and place a piece of dry florists' foam inside each one. Take several clumps of wired pink miniature sunray and insert them in the first basket, keeping the flowers close to the foam so that they almost cover it.

Among the sunray place small pieces of *Leucodendron brunia* to give a contrasting texture. These, along with the sunray, should virtually fill the basket.

Next, bunch together some fluffy heads of rabbit's or hare's tail grass. Keep them taller than the other flowers so that, when slotted in, they rise above the outline.

Finally, make some little bows from pink satin ribbon (following the instructions on page 9) and place one bow on each side of the basket. All three baskets are completed in exactly the same way.

Once the three baskets are finished, tie a piece of co-ordinating cord to each basket handle. Tie all the cords together at the top so that the baskets hang one beneath the other and complete with another pink satin bow.

Create a completely festive atmosphere in your home this Christmas with some of the original and stunning ideas featured in this chapter. We show you how to decorate the focal point of the room: the Christmas tree; and, if you are tired of ordinary tinsel and baubles, we demonstrate how easy it is to exercise individual style and chic at relatively little cost. There are numerous tree decorations to make, as well as unusual festive wreaths and garlands. And for the Christmas and New Year dinner table we show you how to create party crackers and a selection of perfect centrepieces which will complete the most special of meals.

ALL THAT GLITTERS

For a stunning effect this Christmas, choose a colour scheme for your tree and bedeck it in reds and golds, pinks and silvers, or blues and purples, matching it to the decor of your room or simply going for your favourite colours.

Alternatively, for a cool and elegant look such as that shown below, choose only translucent and pearly white decorations, allowing the natural colours of your tree to shine forth.

Of course, it can be quite a costly affair buying all the baubles and beads needed to dress a tree. By covering your tree in colourful bows cut from sparkling party fabric (see right), you can create a lavish effect as well as keep the cost down. You will need about 1.3m (4ft) each of red and gold fabric to dress a medium sized tree, cut into strips 12cm x 80cm (5in x 30in). Fold the raw edges in to the centre along the length of a strip and tie the fabric around the end of a branch, finishing off with a bow. Pull the raw edges out from inside the loops to give the bow more volume and cut the tails in a V shape. Tie as many bows as you like all over the tree, making a large double one to fit on the top. Fill in the gaps with red and gold baubles and drape gold beads elegantly around the tree to finish.

NATURAL BRILLIANCE

STARS AND BOWS

Dried flowers always look beautiful but are especially decorative at Christmas. Brighten up the Christmas tree with sprays of dried flowers tied with tartan ribbon. Choose warm red, russet and golden yellow coloured foliage and as bright a coloured tartan as you can find so that the colours will stand out against the tree. Balance the flowers amongst the branches.

Tie a larger spray upside down at the top of the tree. Next, tie together some cinnamon sticks with tartan ribbon and hang them from the branches on fine thread. As a finishing touch, hang fir cones on narrow ribbons. Stand the tree in a basketwork pot decorated with dried flower heads glued around the rim and tartan ribbon fastened with fine wire.

This tree's stunning effect is easy to achieve. Cut star shapes from silver cardboard (see template on page 95) and position them between the branches. Then make bows from pink paper rope and place them in the gaps. The trimmings can also be hung on fine thread if the branches are rather sparse. Top the tree with a large silver star, attached with a length of wire taped to the back.

For the bows, cut a 33cm (13in) length of paper rope or use a 10cm (4in) wide crepe paper strip; bend the ends to the centre and tightly bind with sticky tape. Cut a 20cm (8in) length for the tails. Bend in half and squeeze the centre, then stick behind the bow. Bind the tails to the bow with a narrow strip and trim the tail ends diagonally. To finish, cover the tub with crepe paper.

ick glittery fabrics and Christmas prints for this simple but effective wreath. Cut out lots of 8cm (3¼in) fabric squares with pinking shears. Cut a 10cm (4in) length of wire and thread a 1cm (³⁄₈in) glass bead in the centre. Pinch a square of fabric together across the diagonal and bend the wire in half across it, twisting the ends together to secure. Repeat for the other fabric squares.

Press the decorations into a dry foam polystyrene wreath, covering it completely (above). To finish, form a double bow from 3.5 cm (1½in) wide silver ribbon and secure onto the ring with wired beads (below). Cut the ribbon ends into Vs.

Dazzle your guests with an everlasting topiary tree in shades of silver and blue. Make up some plaster of Paris and fill a 12cm (5in) diameter plastic flower pot. Hold a 36cm (14in) length of 15mm (⁵⁄₈in) diameter dowel in the centre until set. Then spray the pot and the top of the plaster with silver paint.

Wind an 80cm (32in) length of silver ribbon around the dowel, fastening both ends with double-sided adhesive tape. Push a 20cm (8in) diameter florists' dry foam ball centrally on to the top of the dowel, gouging a hole in the ball first with a craft knife.

Next, make up a selection of decorations from natural materials. Stick short lengths of wire into walnuts and spray them silver. Wind lengths of wire around the base of some fir cones and spray the tips of the cones silver. Cut cinnamon sticks into 5cm (2in) lengths, wire them into bundles of three or four, then wrap the bundles with knotted silver cord to cover the wire.

Using pinking shears, cut out 10cm (4in) squares of glittery and tartan fabrics. Cut a 20cm (8in) length of wire; fold evenly in half across the diagonal of a fabric square, pinching the fabric together, then twist the ends of the wire secure. Repeat for the other fabric pieces. Stick glittery balls onto short lengths of wire.

Press the decorations into the ball until it is completely covered. We have also added artificial berries, silver acorns, wire springs and poppy seed heads. Cover an earthenware flower pot with fabric using PVA adhesive, finishing at the top with a strip of silver ribbon and a bow. Fit the plastic pot inside and a double bow of silver and tartan ribbon around the centre of the stalk.

You will need 60 cm (24 in) red felt and a strip of white fur 49 cm (19½ in) long and 7 cm (2¾ in) wide. You will also need some red ribbon to make a hanging loop. Cut the red felt into a stocking shape.

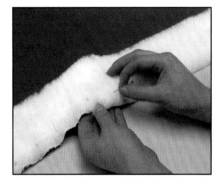

Carefully pin the strip of fur along the top edge of the felt stocking.

Machine (or hand-sew) the fur onto the felt. Sew on a ribbon loop for hanging, then sew up the front and foot part of the stocking.

Using a hot glue gun, attach some spruce, pine cones, dried gypsophila and Christmas tree bells to the stocking. Finally sew on a ribbon bow.

A CHRISTMAS CRACKER

A CHRISTMAS NUT BALL

Assemble some gilded nigella heads, grasses, dried sea lavender and beech masts or cones. You will also need some gold ribbon or cord. Either make a plain cracker of your own or use a sparsely decorated bought one.

Take a pre-formed sphere of dried flower foam. Make a long loop with some ribbon and twist a reasonably long length of wire around the base of the loop, leaving a 'leg' to go through the ball. Pass the wire through the ball until the base of the loop is embedded in the foam. Trim the wire to within 1 cm (½ in) and bend it back into the foam.

Using a hot glue gun, attach the ingredients to one side of the cracker.

Using a hot glue gun, glue a selection of nuts onto the foam, being fairly liberal with the glue.

Once you are happy with the design, add some tiny loops of gold ribbon or cord, making sure that the base of each loop is well hidden.

Once the ball is completely covered with nuts, check for glimpses of the grey foam and, if there are any, cover them with some dried nigella seed heads. Spray the ball well with a polyurethane matt or satin varnish.

HANGING EVERGREEN WREATH

Add several sprigs of holly, again securing them with wire. If the holly is a bit short of berries, you can add some fake berries at this point.

To hang the wreath you will need two lengths of satin ribbon. Each piece should be twice the length of the drop from the ceiling to your hanging height, plus an extra 20cm (8in) for tying around the wreath. Tie each of the four ends opposite one another around the wreath so that the two lengths cross in the centre.

Make four bows from the same colour ribbon and pin them to the wreath over the four tying-on points.

Gently push a length of florist's wire through each of four red wax candles, approximately 1.5cm (½in) above the bases, as shown.

This festive wreath is ideal if you're short of space on the table — it can be suspended from a hook screwed into the ceiling. Use wire cutters to snip the hook off a coat hanger. Bend the hanger into a circular shape. Bunch damp sphagnum moss around the wire to a thickness of about 5cm (2in), using gardener's wire around it to hold it in place.

Take several bushy branches of evergreen, such as cypress, and arrange them to cover the circlet of moss, overlapping the pieces to cover any stalks. Tie the branches to the ring with gardener's twine or wire.

Position each candle halfway between two bows, and twist the wire around the wreath to hold it in place. To hang the wreath, tie another length of ribbon around the two main ribbons where they cross, make a loop to go over the hook, and tie the ends in a bow.

This festive table centrepiece is inexpensive to produce as the foliage used can be found in abundance during the Christmas period. Take a florists' foam ring and insert four candle holders evenly spaced around it.

Dampen the ring and insert four red candles in the holders. We have used hand-made candles for added interest. Now push sprigs of yew into the ring, positioning all the foliage in the same direction.

Next, take four large fir cones and bind wire around the base between the lower scales leaving a long length of wire to insert into the ring. Push the cone wires into the ring between the candles.

Finally, add sprigs of holly and berries to the ring. Berries can be added separately to add colour evenly throughout the decoration. Artificial berries can be used if real ones are not available.

CHRISTMAS BELLS

PATCHWORK STARS

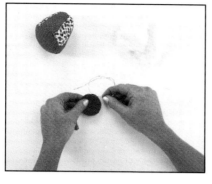

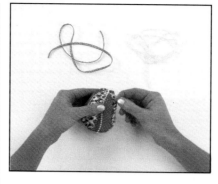

Ring out the bells this Christmas from the tree tops. Using the pattern on page 95, cut out three side panel pieces from each of two festive fabrics. Pin and stitch the panels together, with right sides facing, to form a ring, alternating the fabrics. Cut an 8cm (3¹/₈in) diameter circle for the base and, with right sides facing, sew in place.

Turn the bell the right side out through the open end and fill with shredded wadding. Turn in the top raw edges and work a gathering stitch around the top; pull up tight to close and fasten off. Cut a 4.5cm (1³/₄in) diameter red felt circle for the clapper. Sew running stitch around the outer edge; fill with wadding and gather into a ball; fasten off. Stitch the clapper to the centre of the base.

To decorate the bell, stitch bead trim over the seamlines, beginning and ending at the edge of the base. Finally, tie a 50cm (20in) length of ribbon into a loop and tie the ends into a bow; sew onto the top of the bell.

Eight-pointed stars are a traditional Christmas design. For each side of a star, cut eight diamonds from iron-on interfacing (see page 95 for pattern). Cut two diamonds from each of four fabrics, adding a seam allowance. Fuse interfacings to the fabric diamonds and tack (baste) the raw edges over the interfacing. Oversew the diamonds together to form a star.

Make up two sides in this way and place with wrong sides facing; slip-stitch the outer edges together. Sew four lengths of braid across the seamlines, finishing one off to form a hanging loop. Finally, sew a pearl button to each point and to each indent.

WOVEN CIRCLES

FELT HEARTS

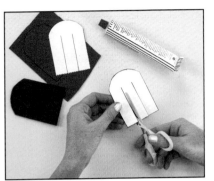

I nterweave red and green felt
shapes to form hearts, adding
glittery beads and sequins. Cut two
templates (see page 95) from thin
cardboard. Stick green felt onto one
side of a template and trim to the
card edges. Cut along the marked
slits. Cover the opposite side of the
template with green felt in the same
way. Repeat the procedure, covering
the second template with red felt.

Interlock the two shapes together by
weaving the strips over and under
their opposite number to form a
heart shape.

U se shiny strands of raffia and
plastic canvas circles (available
from craft shops) to create these
unusual tree ornaments. Weave raffia
over the inner half of a 7.5cm (3in)
circle with straight stitches, working
each quarter section from the same
central hole. The stitches will look
the same from either side.

Punch a hole centrally in the top of
the heart; thread with a 20cm (8in)
length of gold cord and tie into a
loop. Finally, decorate each side of
the heart with sequins and beads;
either glue or handsew them in
place.

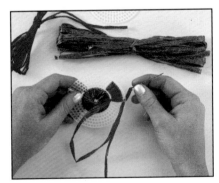

Work the outer half of the circle in
the same way using the second
colour. Blanket stitch around the
outer edge of the circle using the
same colour as the centre, tying the
ends to form a loop.

On each side, handsew pearl bead
trim between the two halves of the
straight stitches and around the outer
edge. Sew a pearl button to the
centre on each side. To finish, tie a
silver ribbon bow around the base of
the loop.

VINE GARLAND CANDLE RING

Gold and silver look stunning by candlelight and this festive arrangement will flatter any table setting. To begin, spray a vine garland with gold paint, sprinkle with gold glitter, and leave to dry.

Take three flat-based candle holders and stick florists' fixative putty under each one. Position them evenly around the garland, using florists' wire to secure each holder firmly in place.

To make the silver roses cut strips of silver crepe paper 53cm (21in) by 9cm (3½in). Fold in half lengthways and tuck the short ends in. Run double-sided tape along the lower edge of a folded strip and place a wired group of gold balls at one end. Roll the crepe paper around the balls, pinching the paper tightly together at the base. Finally, crimp the petal edges to curve outwards.

Stick a double-sided adhesive pad to the base of each rose and position four flowers around each candle holder. Cut 23cm (9in) lengths of gold ribbon and fold into double loops. Secure the ends with florists' wire and stick between the roses using adhesive pads. Tease the rose petals and gold loops to shape to hide the holders and put candles in place.

INCOGNITO

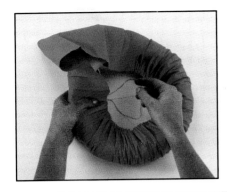

Adorn the New Year dinner table with this attractive centrepiece. Cut a length of crepe paper 120cm x 20cm (48in x 8in). Stick the ends together on the wrong side with clear sticky tape. Place a 25cm (10in) diameter polystyrene ring in the middle and sew the long edges of crepe paper together with a running stitch enclosing the polystyrene ring. Gather up the seam and fasten off.

Spray five candle holders white and push into the ring evenly spaced apart. Then drape strings of white pearls and narrow green coiled giftwrapping ribbon around the ring, gluing the ends to the underside.

Stick two rectangles of metallic blue cardboard back to back with spray adhesive and cut out five masks copying the shape of those shown above and bending backwards. Alternatively metallic, coloured masks can be purchased at stationers and department stores during the festive season. Stick each mask by the tabs, in front of a candle.

Glue tiny blue and green star-shaped sequins to the ring, then cut out ten small stars from silver cardboard and glue between the candles and to each mask. Finally, place silver candles in the holders.

GARDEN ROOM TEMPLATES

One Square represents 2.5cm (1in)

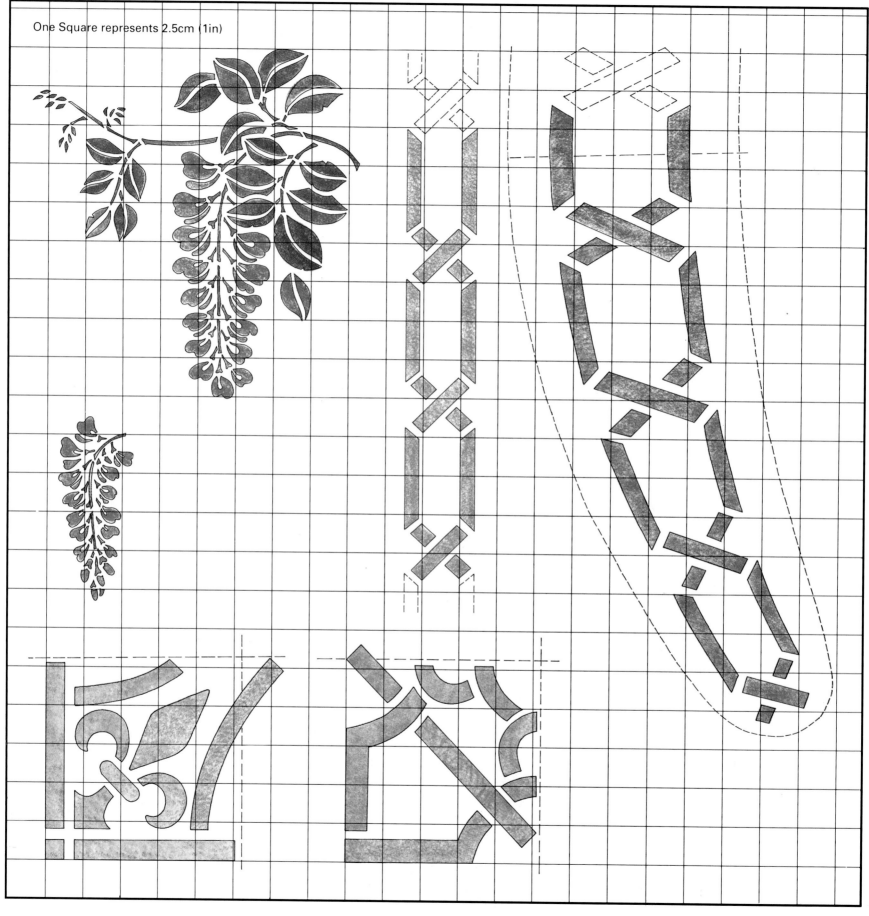

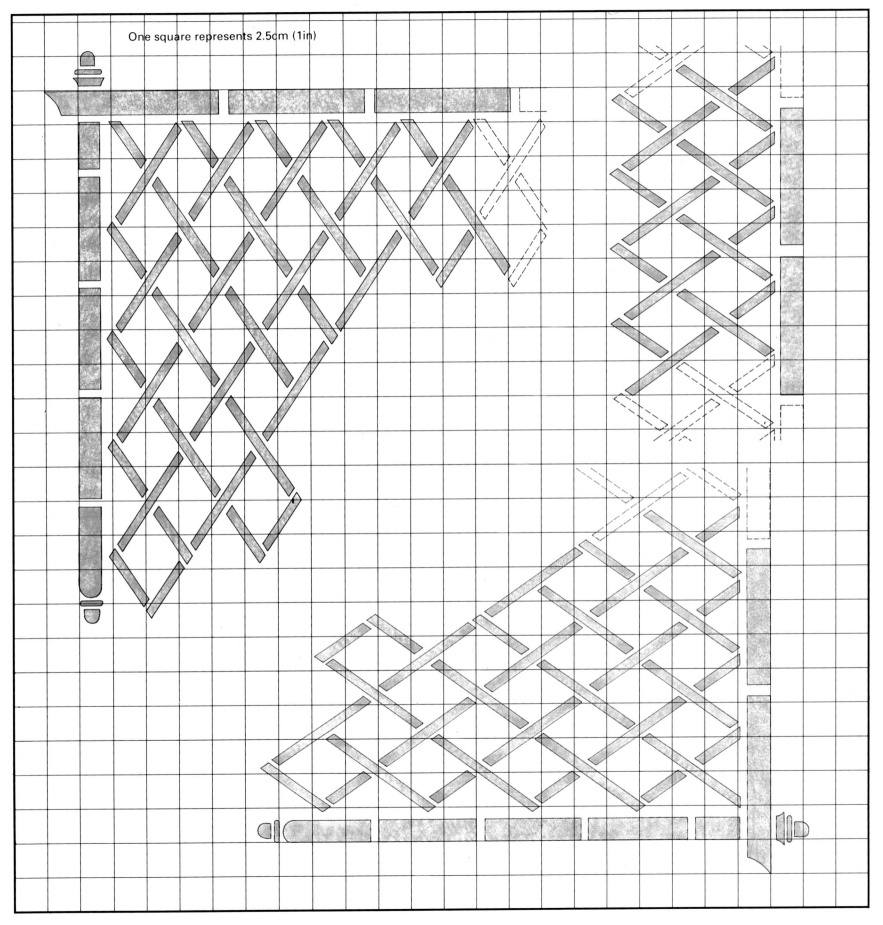

One square represents 2.5cm (1in)

TEMPLATES DESIGN

The design templates on these pages are printed on grids to help you copy them more easily. To reproduce the designs at the required size, refer to the step-by-step instructions on squaring up which can be found on page 7.

Tutti-Frutti Tiles (page 21)
Size as required

Everything's Coming Up Roses (page 31)
Size as required

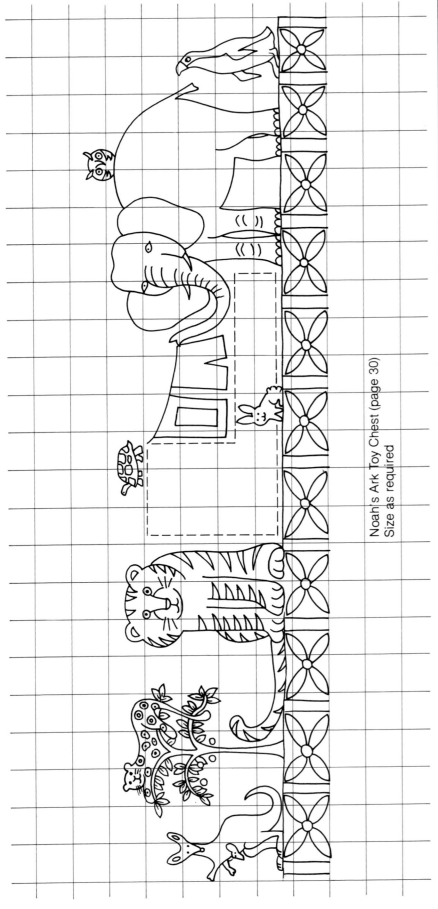

Noah's Ark Toy Chest (page 30)
Size as required

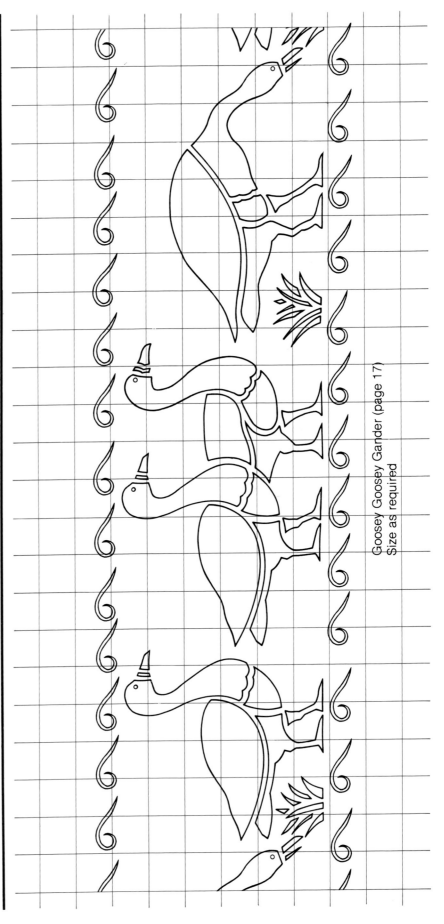

Goosey Goosey Gander (page 17)
Size as required

Stencilled Flowerpiece (page 42)

Suggested size: One
square represents 1.5cm ($^5/_8$in)

Deep Sea Deck Chair (page 32)

Stencilled Flowerpiece (page 42)

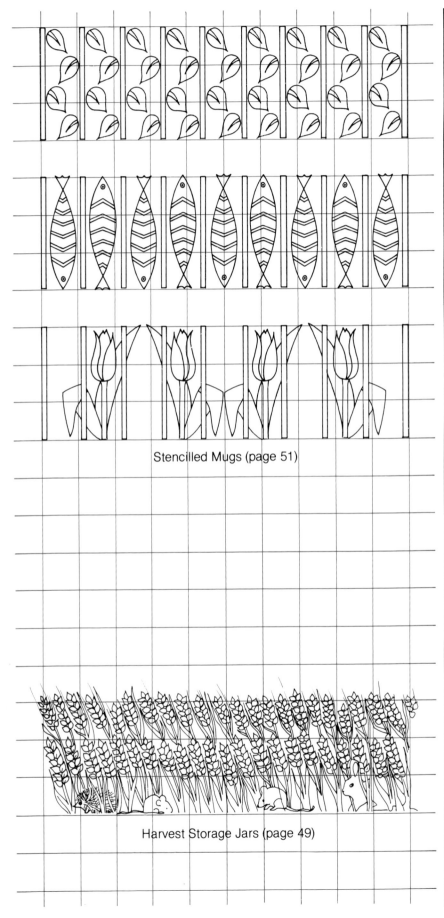

Stencilled Mugs (page 51)

Harvest Storage Jars (page 49)

Size up the templates below as follows: draw up a grid of 2.5cm (1in) squares, then copy the design onto your grid, square by square, using the grid lines as a guide.

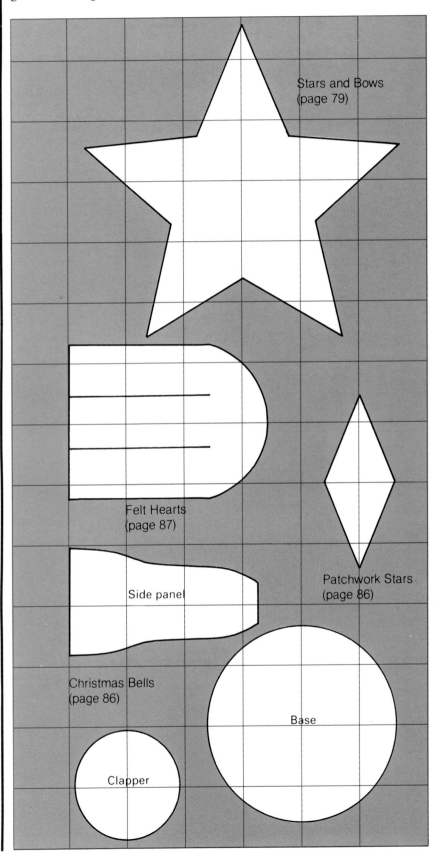

Stars and Bows (page 79)

Felt Hearts (page 87)

Patchwork Stars (page 86)

Side panel

Christmas Bells (page 86)

Base

Clapper

INDEX